EVERYTHING A 13 YEAR OLD SHOULD KNOW

(But Won't Learn at School)

100+ Essential Life Skills for Self-Confidence, Happiness, and Success

FERNE BOWE

Copyright © 2025 Ferne Bowe

Published by: Bemberton Ltd

All rights reserved. No part of this book or any portion thereof may be reproduced in any form by any electronic or mechanical means, without permission in writing from the publisher, except for the use of brief quotes in a book review.

The publisher accepts no legal responsibility for any action taken by the reader, including but not limited to financial losses or damages, both directly or indirectly incurred as a result of the content in this book.

ISBN: 978-1-915833-70-9

Disclaimer: The information in this book is general and designed to be for information only. While every effort has been made to ensure it is wholly accurate and complete, it is for general information only. It is not intended, nor should it be taken as professional advice. The author gives no warranties or undertakings whatsoever concerning the content. For matters of a medical nature, the reader should consult a doctor or other health care professional for specific health-related advice. The reader accepts that the author is not responsible for any action, including but not limited to losses both directly or indirectly incurred by the reader as a result of the content in this book.

View all our books at **bemberton.com**

CONTENTS

5   Introduction

7   Everyday Independence

43 Money and the Economy

65 Emotional Growth and Social Skills

93 Navigating the Social World

117 Digital Life

137 Big-Picture Thinking

159 Conclusion

161 Appendix

BEMBERTON
BOOKS

SOMETHING
FOR YOU

Thanks for buying this book. To show our appreciation, here's a **FREE** printable copy of the "Life Skills for Tweens Workbook"

WITH OVER 80 FUN ACTIVITIES **JUST FOR TWEENS!**

Scan the code to download your FREE printable copy

INTRODUCTION

Welcome to your teenage years!

You're at a point in life when things are changing — fast. Sure, there's excitement about growing up and becoming more independent. But you might also feel overwhelmed. Maybe you've noticed that adults expect more from you now or that friendships feel more complicated. Or you might be figuring out how to balance school, family, and everything else life throws your way. It can be a lot.

The good news? You don't have to figure it out on your own.

This book is here to help you navigate all the stuff that matters but doesn't always get taught in school. We're going to talk about friendships, emotions, independence, decision-making, handling money, and even planning for the future. You'll learn to set boundaries, manage stress, stand up for yourself, and make choices that align with the person you want to be. It won't tell you exactly what to do in every situation, but it *will* give you the tools to **think critically, problem-solve, and make smart decisions**.

How to Use This Book

You don't have to read this cover to cover or all in one sitting. It's meant to be a resource you can return to whenever you need advice or perspective. Each chapter focuses on a different area of life, so if you're struggling with friendships, jump to that section. If you want to get better at managing your time, check out the chapter on goal-setting and productivity.

If something sparks an idea or helps you see things in a new way, take a moment to think about it, write it down, or talk to someone about it. The more you engage with what you're reading, the more useful it will be.

Life doesn't come with a manual, but this book is the next best thing. No boring lectures, no fluff, just real talk to help you feel more confident, capable, and in control. Let's get started!

EVERYDAY INDEPENDENCE

We live in a world that's changing fast, with new technology popping up all the time. It's easy to get caught up in learning digital skills — but what about the **everyday practical skills** that help you navigate life?

For example, in just one day you need to:

- Have clean clothes.
- Eat something (hopefully not just chips).
- Manage your time and schedule.
- And plenty more!

Chances are, your parents still handle a lot of this for you. But as you get older, it's time to take on more responsibility. Learning practical life skills — like cooking, cleaning, and figuring out public transport — helps you become more independent and confident.

But because school is focused on algebra and essays, you might not have picked these skills up yet.

And that's OK. You don't know what you don't know! If you can't tell a spatula from a whisk or have no clue how to reset the WiFi router, don't stress — this is your chance to learn.

This chapter is all about essential life skills that often get skipped at school. From kitchen basics to tackling everyday challenges, this is your starting point. Use this section as a jumping-off point to get more curious about the skills you'll need as you grow.

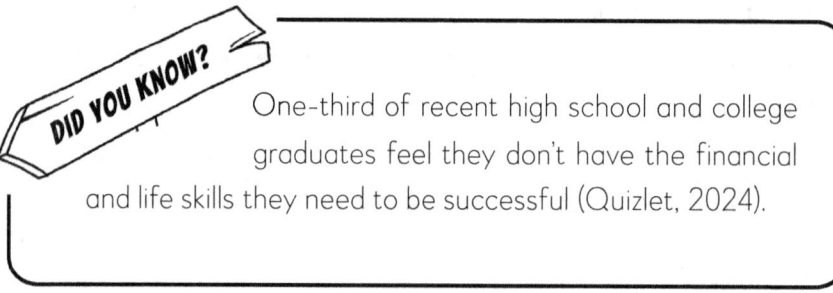

DID YOU KNOW? One-third of recent high school and college graduates feel they don't have the financial and life skills they need to be successful (Quizlet, 2024).

In the Kitchen

How is your cooking? Maybe you're a pro in the kitchen, maybe your specialty is instant noodles, or maybe you've never even boiled water.

Hey! There's no judgment here!

But learning how to cook your own meals is a key life skill — and it helps you make healthier food choices. This is the perfect time to get the basics down. Here are some skills you'll want to master:

- Planning a menu.
- Writing a shopping list.
- Multitasking in the kitchen.
- Following a recipe.

Use this section to get some practice at each of these skills.

DID YOU KNOW?

Learning to cook can actually help you learn coding! Both require creativity and a solid grasp of the basics. Once you understand the fundamentals, you can experiment with different "ingredients" to create something entirely new.

BASIC KITCHEN TERMS

Cooking comes with its own language, and understanding these basic terms will help you get amazing results. Here are a few you'll see often in recipes:

- **Preheat:** This means getting your oven or pan warm before you start cooking.

- **Sauté:** A fancy term for cooking food quickly in a pan with a little oil or butter over medium heat.
- **Simmer:** Cooking something in liquid that is just about boiling, with small bubbles that rise slowly.
- **Whisk:** Mixing ingredients together using a whisk or fork.
- **Dice:** Cutting something into tiny, even-sized cubes.
- **Season:** Adding salt, pepper, or spices/herbs to bring your dish to life.
- **Stir:** Mixing something fairly quickly, usually with a spoon or spatula — think of stirring a pot of soup.
- **Fold:** A gentler mixing technique used for thicker mixes, like when folding whipped cream into batter. The goal is not to deflate the air bubbles.

Essential Kitchen Equipment

With just a few tools, you can get creative and start making delicious meals! You don't need everything on this list right away, but these items will definitely come in handy:

- **Sharp knife:** Your go-to tool for chopping, slicing, and dicing.
- **Cutting board:** A safe surface to chop food on (wood or glass is best).
- **Nonstick pan:** Perfect for cooking eggs, grilled cheese, and other stovetop favorites.
- **Saucepan:** Great for boiling pasta, making sauces, or simmering soups.
- **Mixing bowls:** For whisking, mixing, or holding ingredients.

- **Whisk or fork:** For beating eggs or mixing sauces.
- **Measuring cups and spoons:** For using the right amount of ingredients.
- **Spatula:** A flexible tool for flipping, stirring, or scraping.
- **Tongs:** Handy for flipping food or grabbing items out of boiling water.
- **Colander:** For draining pasta or washing fruits and vegetables.
- **Wooden spoon:** Perfect for mixing and stirring.

Cooking Basics: Eggs Five Ways

If the thought of learning to cook is freaking you out, **eggs are the perfect place to start**. They're versatile, healthy, delicious, and — best of all — super easy to cook!

Hard Boiled Eggs

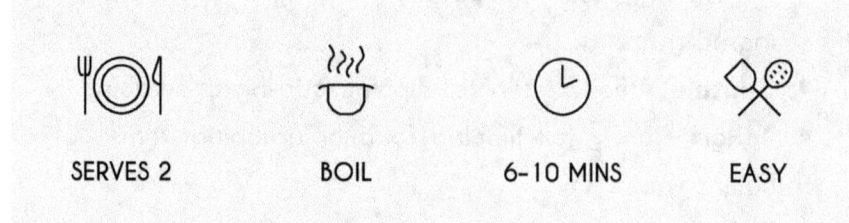

SERVES 2　　　BOIL　　　6-10 MINS　　　EASY

Equipment: *Saucepan, timer, tongs*

1. Fill a saucepan with water and bring it to a boil (you should see lots of bubbles in about five minutes).

2. Gently add the eggs and cook for:
   - **6 minutes** for a soft yolk.
   - **10 minutes** for a fully cooked yolk.

3. Use tongs to transfer the eggs into a bowl of cold water for a few minutes.

4. Gently tap the eggs on a hard surface to crack the shell, then peel it off.

Pro tip: *Older eggs (not too old!) are easier to peel.*

Fried Eggs

SERVES 1   FRY   5-7 MINS   EASY

Equipment: *Nonstick pan, spatula*

1. Heat a little oil or butter in a pan over medium heat.
2. Carefully crack an egg directly into the pan. Try not to break the yolk!
3. Fry until the edges of the white are crispy and the yolk is set (not too jiggly).

Pro tip: *For an "over-easy" egg, flip it gently and cook for another 30 seconds.*

Scrambled Eggs

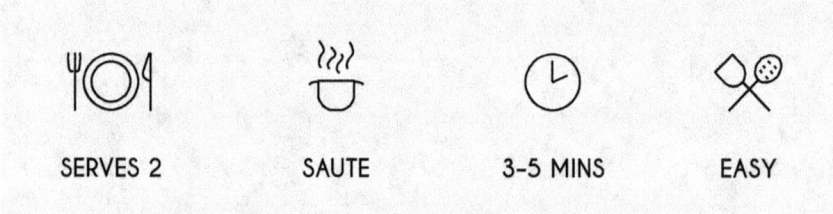

SERVES 2   **SAUTE**   **3-5 MINS**   **EASY**

Equipment: *Bowl, whisk, nonstick pan, spatula*

1. Crack two or three eggs into a bowl and whisk with a pinch of salt and pepper.
2. Heat butter in a pan over a low heat, then pour in the eggs.
3. Stir the mixture gently with a spatula until the eggs are creamy.

Pro tip: *Add a splash of milk or cream while whisking for extra fluffiness.*

Omelet

| SERVES 1 | FRY | 4-6 MINS | MODERATE |

Equipment: *Bowl, whisk, nonstick pan, spatula*

1. Whisk two eggs with a pinch of salt and pepper.
2. Pour the mixture into a hot pan and let it cook undisturbed. You'll see the edges start to set.
3. Add your favorite fillings (like cheese, veggies, or ham) to one side.
4. Use the spatula to fold the omelet in half. If it is properly set, it will fold easily.
5. Cook for another two to three minutes.

Pro tip: *Use a low heat to avoid burning the bottom.*

Poached Eggs
(slightly more advanced)

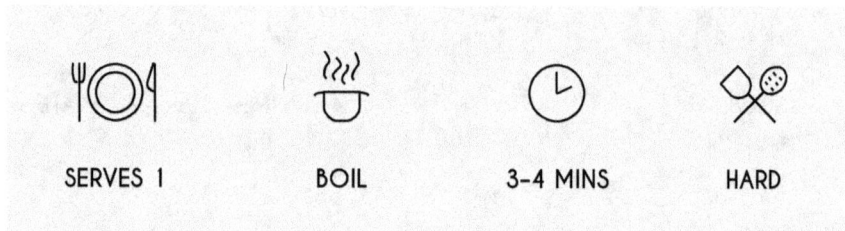

SERVES 1 **BOIL** **3-4 MINS** **HARD**

Equipment: *Saucepan, slotted spoon*

1. Bring a saucepan of water to a gentle simmer (lots of small bubbles).
2. Add a splash of vinegar (one teaspoon per cup of water).
3. Carefully stir the water with a spoon to create a "whirlpool."
4. Crack an egg into the center of the whirlpool and cook for four minutes.
5. Use a slotted spoon to gently lift the egg out.

Pro tip: *Fresh eggs work better when poaching.*

Three Simple Meals to Master

With these three easy dishes under your belt, you'll always have a delicious meal within reach. And once you've got the basics down, you can start experimenting with different ingredients to make them your own!

Grilled Cheese Sandwich

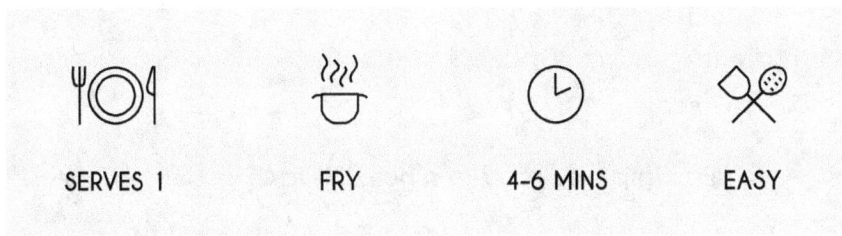

SERVES 1 | FRY | 4-6 MINS | EASY

Equipment: *Nonstick pan, spatula, knife, chopping board*

Ingredients: *Butter, sliced bread, cheese*

1. Spread butter on one side of each slice of bread.
2. Put a slice or two of cheese between the unbuttered sides, so the butter faces out.
3. Heat a pan over medium heat (not too hot, or the bread will burn!).
4. Place the sandwich in the pan and cook for two to three minutes on each side until the bread turns golden and crispy and the cheese melts.

Basic Pasta with Sauce

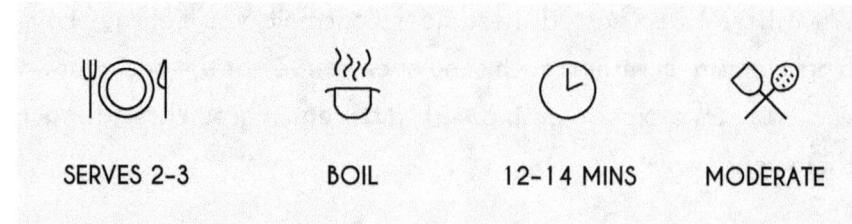

SERVES 2-3 BOIL 12-14 MINS MODERATE

Equipment: *Large saucepan, colander, wooden spoon/spatula, wide pan or wok*

Ingredients: *Pasta, salt, pasta sauce or olive oil, garlic powder, and Parmesan cheese*

1. Bring a big pot of water to a boil (this takes about 10 minutes).

2. Add one teaspoon of salt to the water and add your pasta. Give it a stir so it doesn't stick together.

3. Cook for about 10 minutes (check the package for the exact time). Taste to check it's done — it should be soft but not too mushy.

4. Drain the pasta using a colander — careful, the water and steam will be hot!

5. Transfer the pasta back to the pot or into a wide pan over *low heat*.

6. Pour in a jar of pasta sauce or mix in olive oil, a sprinkle of garlic powder, and Parmesan cheese. Stir and cook for another minute or two.

Veggie Stir-Fry

SERVES 2-3 FRY 15-20 MINS MODERATE

Equipment: *Chopping board, sharp knife, wide pan or wok*

Ingredients: *Mix of veggies, sunflower, vegetable, or sesame oil, soy or teriyaki sauce, leftover/pre-prepared rice or noodles*

1. Chop up your favorite vegetables (bell peppers, zucchini, broccoli, and cauliflower work well).

2. Heat a tablespoon of oil in a pan over medium heat.

3. Add the veggies and stir them around for about five to seven minutes, until they're slightly soft but still a little crunchy.

4. Pour in a splash of soy sauce or teriyaki sauce and mix everything up. Taste and add more sauce if needed. Remember, you can always add more but can't take it out, so go slowly!

5. Serve the veggies over rice or noodles. You can use leftover rice or noodles, or start cooking them before chopping the veggies.

Washing Up

Washing up after cooking might not be the most exciting part of making a meal, but it's a super important step.

Start by clearing away any leftovers or food scraps, and then fill your sink with warm, soapy water. Wash the dishes using a sponge or scrub brush. Don't forget to rinse everything well to get rid of soap. Then, either dry your dishes with a clean towel or let them air dry. It might feel like a lot at first, but once you get into the habit, it becomes second nature — and you'll always have a clean kitchen ready for your next meal.

Home Hacks

Being independent isn't just about cooking eggs or unlocking your phone after forgetting the passcode (again). It's also about **handling everyday situations** — like knowing what to do when the shower is overflowing instead of yelling, *"Mooooom!"*

This section will teach you simple but essential skills that will help you solve problems and take care of the space around you.

LAUNDRY 101

You're definitely old enough to start washing your own clothes — just think, no more digging through piles or asking *"Where's my hoodie?"* Laundry is actually pretty easy, but there are a few things to know before you get started.

Get It Sorted

You might be tempted to just toss everything into the washing machine, but unless you *want* pink socks or a weirdly splotchy shirt, **sorting your laundry is key. Some colors "run" in the wash**, which means they can stain lighter fabrics. To avoid laundry disasters, separate your clothes into three groups:

- **Whites:** Anything that's mostly white or a very light color (like beige or pale gray).
- **Darks:** Anything that is mainly a dark color, like black or dark blue.
- **Brights:** Bright colors like reds (red loves running!), yellows, and bright greens.

Washing Machine Basics

The washing machine might look complicated, but after a few loads, you'll be a laundry pro! Here's how to do it:

1. **Load it up.** Add your sorted clothes to the machine — just don't overstuff it!

2. **Add detergent.** Check the instructions on the detergent bottle for the right amount.
3. **Choose the right settings:**
   - **Load size:**
     » Small = ¼ full.
     » Medium = ½ full.
     » Large = ¾ full.
     » Extra large = full.
   - **Water temperature:**
     » **Cold:** Best for delicate fabrics and colors.
     » **Warm:** Great for everyday loads.
     » **Hot:** Ideal for towels, bedding and heavily soiled items! (Although some fabrics can get damaged by high heat, so always read the label.)
   - **Cycle setting**

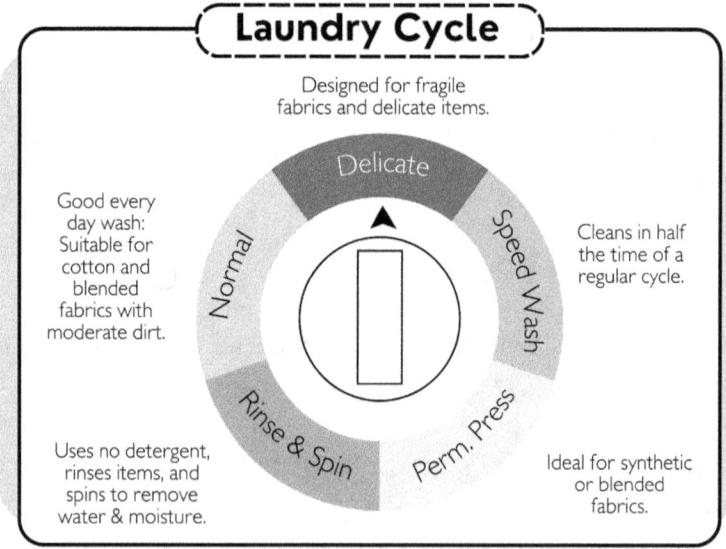

After Washing

When the cycle is finished, take your clean washing out of the machine and put it into a laundry tub. Now, you can either put it into the tumble dryer, hang it on the line outside, or put it on a clothes rack to dry. Once they're dry, fold or hang the clothes up right away to keep everything neat and ready to wear. And don't forget to clean out the lint trap if you're using the dryer!

DRAIN DRAMA

Have you ever found yourself standing in the shower as the water rises around your ankles? Don't worry, it happens to everyone!

Drains get blocked because dirt, hair, and soap gunk build up over time. Unclogging drains is pretty gross but necessary. It's also not as hard as you might think. Here are a couple of ways to fix it:

1. Drain Snake

A drain snake is a simple hand-held tool that slides down into the drain, grabs onto clumps of hair and gunk, and pulls them out. It's kind of gross, but also strangely satisfying.

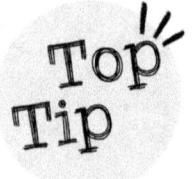

Top Tip: If you don't have a drain snake, you can bend a wire clothes hanger or use a piece of wire to fish out the blockage.

2. Kitchen Solutions

You probably have vinegar and baking soda (sodium bicarbonate) in your pantry, but did you know they're handy for cleaning too? These ingredients work wonders in both the kitchen and bathroom!

Pour one cup of baking soda and one cup of vinegar down the drain. It will bubble and fizz for a while — that means it's working!

Pop the plug in and wait an hour before rinsing the drain with boiling water. The chemical reaction between the vinegar and baking soda helps break down drain gunk and remove dirt buildup. Some blockages might need more than one treatment.

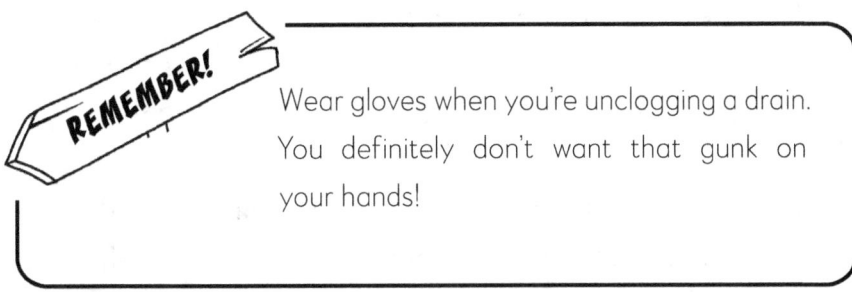

REMEMBER! Wear gloves when you're unclogging a drain. You definitely don't want that gunk on your hands!

From Chaos to Clean

Do you have chores to do? You might think they're a pain or unfair. But doing chores and keeping your room clean are important life skills — we all have to do them!

One day, you might share a house with someone or work in a busy office. Can you imagine what would happen if your desk was always messy or you didn't help wash dishes or take out the trash?

Keeping your space tidy shows respect — for yourself and those around you. And once you make it a habit, it sticks. Try these simple tricks to get started:

The Five-Minute Rule

Set a five-minute timer and **pick up as much trash and stuff** that doesn't belong in your space as possible. You'll be amazed at how much tidying you can do in five minutes!

Create Zones

Break your space into zones — like your desk or cupboard — and tackle one at a time. This way, cleaning won't feel overwhelming.

Make a Playlist

Cleaning, tidying, and organizing don't have to be boring. Create a cleaning playlist with your favorite songs to make it more fun and keep you motivated.

Pack away laundry immediately and do a five-minute tidy every day. That way, cleaning won't pile up or get out of control.

Maintenance Basics

These days, it's easy to pick up the phone and call for help when something needs fixing. But **DIY (do it yourself) skills are really important** — they can help you **save time** (no waiting for jobs to be done) **and money** (no paying people to fix your stuff).

Here are three home projects you can try — with the help of an adult when needed.

Changing a Lightbulb

If you're doing homework and your overhead light or desk lamp stops working, the lightbulb is the most likely culprit. The good news is changing a lightbulb is easy once you know how!

Different Bulb Types

But first... Did you know there are different types of light bulbs and fittings? The type of bulb will affect how you remove or fit it. There are two types of bulb fittings — screw-in and bayonet, and each comes in different sizes. Screw-in bulbs are the most common.

- **Screw-in:** To remove, gently twist the bulb to the left (counterclockwise). Fit a new bulb by twisting it to the right (clockwise).

- **Bayonet:** Push down gently and twist left to remove. To fit a new one, push down gently and twist right.

Brightness and Wattage

- **Lumens** measure the brightness of the bulb (**the more lumens, the brighter the bulb**).
- **Wattage** tells you how much energy the bulb uses. Traditionally, higher-wattage bulbs were brighter and used more electricity. However, modern LED bulbs use much less wattage to produce the same brightness, making them more energy efficient.

How to Change a Lightbulb

1. First, **turn off the light** at the switch or socket. **This is very important** because it stops the electricity flowing to the light, removing the risk of an electric shock when you change the bulb.
2. Wait a few minutes (the bulb may be hot!).
3. Carefully remove the old bulb from its socket. If you need a ladder, get someone to hold it steady.
4. Insert the new bulb. Make sure it's the same size and brightness, not just the same fitting!

Hanging Pictures

It's easy to use Blu Tack or tape to stick up pictures and posters. But what about a notice board or framed photos? Hanging framed pictures properly makes a room look more put-together — and it's easier than you think!

1. **Choose the right spot.** Hold the picture against the wall and decide where you want it. Mark the top center with a pencil.
2. **Find the hanging point.** Measure the distance from the top of the frame to the hanging wire or bracket, then mark that spot on the wall.
3. **Hammer a nail or insert a hook:**
   - Light picture? Just a nail will work.
   - Heavy picture? Use a wall anchor (a screw inside a plastic plug) to hold it in place. You need to drill a hole first before using a wall anchor — see the section below, and ask an adult for help.
4. **Hang the picture.** Place the wire or bracket over the nail or hook.

Using a Drill

To hang heavier pictures or other items, you might need to use a wall anchor. This means using a drill, which can be dangerous, so get an adult to help you.

1. **Mark the wall** where you want the screw.
2. **Select a drill bit** that matches the size of your wall anchor.

3. **Hold the drill straight and gently drill** into the wall where you made your mark. Make sure to drill deep enough for the anchor to fit snugly.
4. **Push the anchor** into the hole — it should sit flush with the wall. You may need to tap it in with a hammer.
5. Now that the anchor is in place, you can **insert a screw** into it. Tighten it with a screwdriver.
6. **Hang your item**.

CLEANING THE SHOWER HEAD

Nothing is more irritating than dancing around in the shower because of clogged nozzles. So, if your shower spray is wonky, here's how to fix it:

1. **Fill a plastic bag with vinegar** and secure it over the showerhead with an elastic band. Let it soak for **30 minutes**.
2. **Remove the bag** and use a **toothpick** to clear clogged nozzles. An old toothbrush and baking soda work too.
3. **Run hot water** for a few minutes to flush out loosened dirt and grime.

HANDY DIY TOOLS

Many home maintenance jobs use the same basic tools. Here are a few essentials that will help you with all kinds of projects.

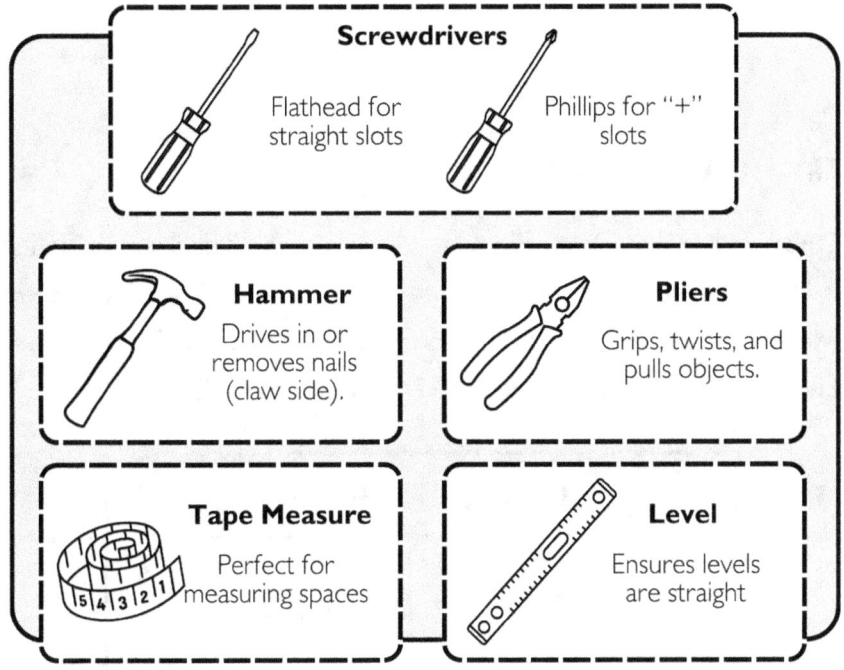

Time Boss: How to Organize Your Day

Time management is like a superpower — it makes life **WAY** less stressful. The great news is it's not something you're born with; it's a skill you can learn, practice, and perfect!

Here's how to get on top of your schedule and make time for the stuff that matters.

Write It Down

A planner, digital calendar, sticky notes...the best option is whatever works for you. Whether you need to remember project deadlines or sports fixtures, **write everything down** so nothing slips through the cracks.

Try the Eisenhower Matrix

Once you've written it all down, you might feel like your to-do list is like a mountain you have no idea how to climb. **The Eisenhower Matrix** is a simple trick to help you figure out **what to do first, what can wait, and what doesn't need to be done at all.**

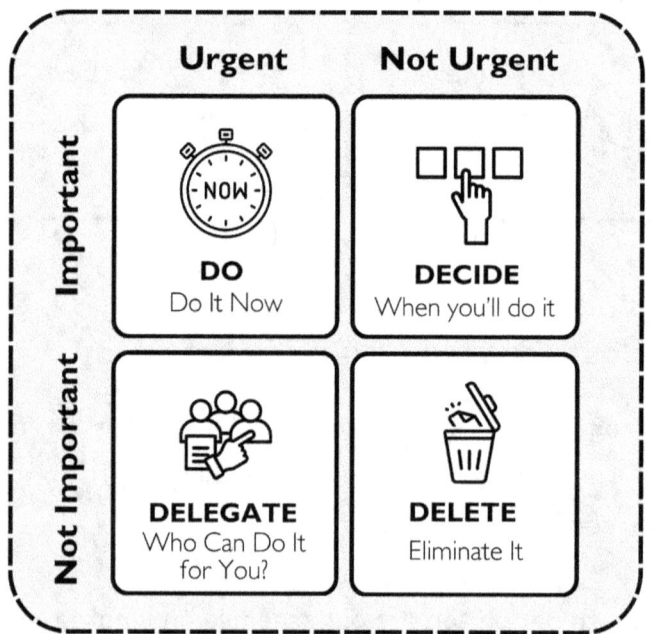

It works by putting your tasks into four categories based on two things:

- ***How urgent is it?*** Does it need to be done right now or very soon?
- ***How important is it?*** Will it make a big difference or help you reach a goal?

1. Urgent + important = do it first

These are your "handle it now" tasks. They're both urgent (time-sensitive) and important (they really matter). Some examples might include:

- Studying for a test that's tomorrow.
- Turning in homework that's due today.

Pro tip: Tackle these first when your energy is high!

2. Important but not urgent = schedule it

These tasks matter **but don't need to be done right away**. Plan them for a specific time in your calendar so they don't sneak up on you. Examples could include:

- Preparing for a project that's due in two weeks.
- Saving up money for a new game console.

Pro tip: These are often the tasks that **make a big difference over time**, so don't ignore them.

3. Urgent but not important = delegate or ask for help

These tasks **need to happen soon** but **don't require your personal genius**. If possible, ask someone else to help out. Examples might include:

- When you're working on a group project, give each person a task instead of doing everything yourself.
- If you're prepping for a group study session, ask a friend to create flashcards while you write the study outline.

Pro tip: It's okay to ask for help — you don't have to do everything yourself!

4. Not urgent + not important = delete or ignore

These tasks are time-wasters. They don't need to be done at all. Some examples could include:

- Watching random YouTube videos.
- Rearranging the posters on your walls (instead of studying).

Pro tip: It can be hard to **say "no" to time-wasting activities**. Don't worry — it gets easier with practice!

Getting Around

What kinds of public transport have you used before? The bus? The train? Taxis? The subway?

Public transport helps you get from place to place, but the different systems can be confusing to use — and maybe even scary. But once you know what you're doing, **public transport is your passport to freedom and confidence!**

Start by planning your route:

1. **Confirm the full address** of your destination using Google Maps. You can even check out a street view photo.
2. **Choose the best transport option.** Buses are great for local routes but can get stuck in traffic. Trains and subways are good for longer distances but may have fewer stops. Taxis are more flexible but can be expensive and also get stuck in traffic.
3. **Look for routes that have fewer transfers** (less swapping from one bus/train to another) so you don't get stressed or confused. If you need to switch buses or trains, check how long it will take to walk between stops.
4. **Arrive a few minutes early** and check for delays.
5. **Have a backup route** (just in case!).

Bus Timetable

From St. Paul's Cathedral to Buckingham Palace

BUS STOPS	DAY TIMES						
St. Paul's Cathedral	08:34	10:12	11:45	13:45	14:30	16:30	18:45
Aldwych	08:46	10:14	11:57	13:57	14:34	16:42	18:48
The City	08:48	10:22	11:59	13:59	14:42	16:44	18:50
London Bridge	08:56	10:29	12:14	14:07	14:44	16:52	18:58
Tower Bridge	09:03	10:38	12:23	14:14	14:52	16:59	19:05
Tower of London	09:12	10:43	12:28	14:23	14:53	17:04	19:14
Embankment	09:17	10:49	12:34	14:28	15:08	17:13	19:19
Big Ben	09:30	10:56	12:41	14:34	15:15	17:19	19:25
Buckingham Palace	09:38	11:04	12:49	14:41	15:19	17:26	19:32

The easiest way to feel confident using public transport is to USE IT! If you need to take a new journey by public transport, consider doing a trial run. Use these tips to help you:

- **Plan your trip**, including a backup plan.
- **Take a friend** for support. Make the trip an adventure!
- **Buy your tickets with an app**, so it's one less thing to worry about.
- **Check the route on Google Maps** and make a note of landmarks.
- **Take cash** and, if you have one, make sure your **phone is fully charged**.
- **Keep a real map** in your bag, just in case!

Finally, here are some **pro tips for public transport:**

- **Know your stop:** You will feel more in control if you know your destination.
- **Have your ticket ready:** Whether you have a physical ticket or use an app, ensure you have the "payment" ready to show to inspectors or scan at terminals.
- **Double-check your directions:** Look for signs that you're going the right way, or ask the conductor/driver.
- **Stay safe:** Keep your belongings close, be mindful of the space you take up, and watch which doors are for entering and exiting.

USING A MAP

Have you ever used a paper map? People don't use them much nowadays because they rely on digital maps. In fact, **over 600 million miles are driven each day using Google Maps** (Lau, 2020). But what if your phone was dead or you were somewhere with patchy service? A map would really come in handy!

Maps aren't as complicated as they look. Here's what you need to know:

- **Title:** Tells you what the map is about (like a city map, hiking trail map, or subway map).

- **Compass rose:** Shows the cardinal directions: north, south, east, and west. **Most maps have north at the top**, but double-check just in case!
- **Key:** Explains what the symbols, colors, and lines on the map mean.
- **Scale:** Shows how distances on the map compare with real life (e.g., "1 inch = 1 mile").
- **Landmarks:** Landmarks, like buildings, mountains, bridges, or statues, can help you get oriented when you're unsure where you are.

Digital Troubleshooting

Technology is amazing — until it stops working! Laggy WiFi, apps crashing or endless updates can derail homework plans or project deadlines. But don't panic — many tech issues have **quick and easy fixes**.

WiFi Issues

Is slow internet driving you nuts? Try these ideas:

- **Move closer to the router.** Walls and closed doors can sometimes block WiFi signals.
- **Disconnect and reconnect** your device to the internet — sometimes, it just needs a reset.

- **Check the router.** Does it have blue, green, or white lights? That's usually a good sign. Red lights or no lights are usually a problem. Try restarting the router:
  » Unplug it.
  » Wait 30 seconds.
  » Plug it back in and wait a few minutes for it to reset.

Apps Acting Weird

If an app freezes or closes suddenly, it probably needs an update. Head to the App Store or Google Play, search for the app, and if an update is available, you'll see the option next to the app name.

If an update isn't available, try:

- **Restarting your device.**
- **Clearing the cache:** Go to the app settings and clear the stored data.
- **Deleting and reinstalling the app.**

Device Updates

Updates can be irritating, but they're vital for keeping your device safe and running smoothly. They can also fix bugs and make your device faster.

- **Go to *Settings* > *System* or *Software Update*.**
- **Check for updates** and follow the instructions.
- **Schedule updates overnight** so they don't disturb your work.

Keyboard or Screen Freeze

There's nothing scarier than your screen freezing in the middle of an assignment. *(**Pro tip:** Use online document software like Google Docs that auto-saves your work. **Second pro tip:** Save your work often and back up your files!)*

- **Restart your device** — this usually solves the problem.
- **Check your storage.** Low space can cause freezing, so clear out unnecessary apps, photos, and files.
- **Close background apps.** Too many apps running at once can slow things down.
- **Check for software updates.** An outdated system can cause crashes.

If your device **keeps freezing**, there may be a bigger issue that needs checking.

Charging Problems

Yes, you could get a new charging cable. But before rushing to the store, try these tips:

- **Check the cable for damage**.
- **Clean the port on your device** with a toothpick (gently!) or a piece of thin plastic. Sometimes it just gets mucky.
- **Try another outlet**. The problem might be the wall socket, not the charger.

Learning Life Skills

If it seems like there's a lot of stuff you don't know yet...that's okay! Life is about learning. Even adults are still learning and figuring things out. The best way to pick up life skills is to **try new things**. Sure, you may burn some eggs or turn your white shirt blue, but **trial and error is how you learn and build confidence** — and hey, blue looks great on you!

MONEY AND THE ECONOMY

Money might seem like a mystery right now. Your parents probably handle most of the big expenses, and you might not know what things cost day-to-day. But understanding money is one of the most valuable life skills you can learn — no matter how much (or how little) you have.

The more you understand how money works, the more **options and freedom** you'll have in life — so, maybe it's time to get curious!

> **DID YOU KNOW?** New research from Junior Achievement USA found that 54% of teens say they feel unprepared to finance their futures (Achievement, 2023).

This chapter covers all the money basics that you need to know. There are no boring lectures, just practical tips to help you feel confident about earning, spending, and saving.

Budgeting 101

Budgeting might not sound exciting, but it's essential. A budget helps you make the most of your money, reducing the chances of wasting or losing it. Think of it as a **plan for your money** — helping you divide what you have between important things like food, gas, and, of course, WiFi.

Although budgeting is important, **it's not complicated**. The hardest part is sticking to it. A budget tells you:

- How much money you have.
- How much money you need.
- How much money you can spend.

Categorizing Your Spending

You'll want to split your budget into **three main categories: essentials, fun stuff, and savings.**

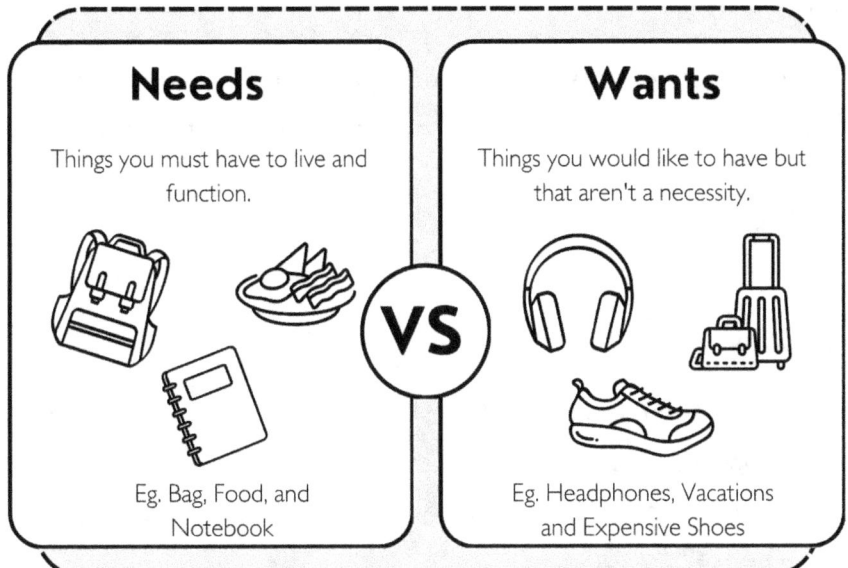

Essentials

These are the things you **need** rather than just **want**. Your parents might cover many of your essential needs, like food, clothing, and toiletries, so your list might be small. An essential for you could be something like your favorite moisturizer or hair gel — something you really don't want to do without.

As an adult, your essentials will look different. **Rent, groceries, car payments, insurance, and utility bills** all become part of the equation.

Fun Stuff

This is probably where most of your spending money goes — things like **video games, books, snacks, movie tickets, or accessories**. Adults also have a fun budget, which might include concerts, hobbies, or dining out.

Savings

This is money you **set aside for later**. At 13, you might save up for a book, earpods, or new shoes. As an adult, savings are crucial. People save for emergencies, their future plans, and big purchases like a house or a car.

CREATING A BUDGET

Do you know how to make your own budget? It's easy:

1. Write down how much money you have right now. Include everything — your allowance, birthday gifts, babysitting money, **whatever you have "coming in."**
2. Spend a week or so **tracking what you spend** your money on. Keep receipts and a written record, or use an app. You can't make a budget if you don't know how much you spend, so include every little thing.
3. **Create your budget**. Below are three different budget options you can try.

50/30/20 Method

Elizabeth Warren's 50/30/20 method is an easy way to start budgeting. Half of your money goes toward essentials, 30% on the fun stuff, and 20% should go into savings.

Pay Yourself First

If you're saving up for something important, then this method works well. Instead of saving last, you **save first.** You're making savings a priority instead of an afterthought. By doing this each time you get money, you'll build a habit.

Zero-Based Budgeting

The idea is to take all the money you have coming in and **give every single dollar a job** — so that by the end, your budget equals zero. With this method, you always know where every cent is going, and nothing slips through the cracks. Plus, it helps you think about your priorities.

For example, if you get $50 a month for allowance or chores, give every dollar a purpose.

- **Essentials:** $20 for things like replacing worn-out earbuds, personal care items, or a birthday gift for a family member.

- **Fun stuff:** $15 for a new book, a game upgrade, or a movie night with friends.
- **Savings:** $10 toward a long-term goal, like a laptop or a bike.
- **Giving:** $5 to donate to a charity.

Budget Worksheet

How much money do you have?		
What do you want to buy?	Item(s)	Cost
"Ensure your spending aligns with your budget"	1. _____	$ _____
	2. _____	$ _____
	3. _____	$ _____
How much will all of this cost?	Total	$
How much money remains?	Subtract the total cost of your items from the money you started with.	$
What will you do with it?	Save ☐	Spend ☐

Stop and Think: If you find managing your money tricky, maybe you need to change how you think about budgeting. It's not always about saying "*no*" to those new shoes or pizza with friends. It's about being able to **say "yes" when it matters**, like saving up for something big or important.

SAVING

Saving money isn't just about putting some cash aside for a rainy day — it's about building a foundation for your future. That might sound dramatic, but saving now will help you develop a good money habit that you'll need as an adult. As a teen, you have a couple of savings options:

- **A piggy bank or cash jar** is great for short-term goals.
- If you want to keep your money secure and maybe even earn a little interest, **a savings account** is the best option.

DID YOU KNOW?

Interest is extra money added to what you save or owe. When you keep money in a bank account, the bank pays you a specific percentage of the total amount as interest. For example, if you put $100 into a savings account that earns 5% interest per year, you'll have $105 after a year.

But it works the other way round, too — you'll pay interest on borrowed money or items bought on credit if you don't pay what you owe on time. Let's say you owe $100 and the interest rate is 20%. That $100 will become $120, then $144, and so on — making the debt harder to pay off.

Saving is a way to give yourself choices in the future. Having backup money to draw on is always a good idea, whether you need it for an emergency or want to spend it on a treat. Saving is easy when you:

- **Stick to your budget.**
- **Add money regularly**, even if it's only a small amount.
- **Avoid spending your savings!**

Tax Basics

What do you know about taxes?

If your answer is **"nothing,"** you're not alone! Plenty of adults don't fully understand taxes either — that's why many hire professionals to handle them. But even if you're not the one filing taxes yet, it's important to know **what they are and why they matter.**

Taxes affect your life in more ways than you might think. They help pay for **smooth roads, parks, emergency services, schools, libraries, and trash collection** — things that make everyday life better. Imagine what life would be like **without** those things!

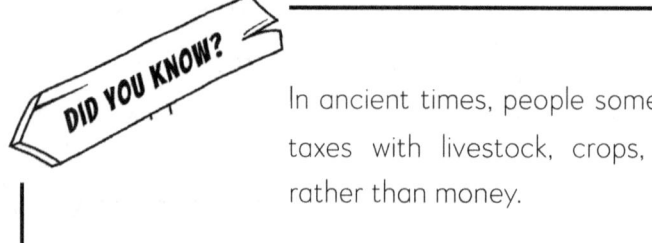

In ancient times, people sometimes paid taxes with livestock, crops, and labor rather than money.

Different Types of Taxes

You'll deal with several different kinds of taxes in your life, so why not get a handle on them now?

Income Tax

When you start earning money, a percentage of it is taken as taxes. But don't worry! You have to earn a certain amount before you start paying taxes.

Sales Tax

Did you know that you're already paying sales tax? Next time you buy a hoodie or a pair of jeans, look at the price on the tag and compare it to what you pay at checkout. The sales tax will probably be added, so you'll pay a bit more.

Value Added Tax (VAT)

Some countries include the sales tax in the price tag instead of adding it at checkout. This is called VAT and varies by country and product type. You'll usually see it listed on the receipt.

Understanding Profit

When you buy something, what you pay doesn't all go into the store owner's pocket. There's much more to it than what's on the price tag!

Let's use a hoodie as an example. A store buys a number of hoodies from the manufacturer at a certain price and then sells them to its customers. The price that it charges is made up of different parts, with only some of it being profit.

Costs

There are the **production costs,** such as the materials (zipper, fabric, thread, etc.) used to make the hoodie. Then, there is the packaging, shipping, and warehouse storage. And don't forget the people who made the hoodie have to be paid. All these costs are factored into the overall **cost of making the hoodie**.

Overheads

Overheads are the **behind-the-scenes business costs** like rent, electricity, staff wages, website costs, and marketing fees. Even if the store sells nothing, it still has to pay these expenses every month.

PROFIT

Once a business has covered the costs, overheads, and taxes, **any money left over is profit**. Profit can be reinvested in the business to help it grow or used for other things. A business that doesn't consistently make a profit might not last long. **No profit = no business!**

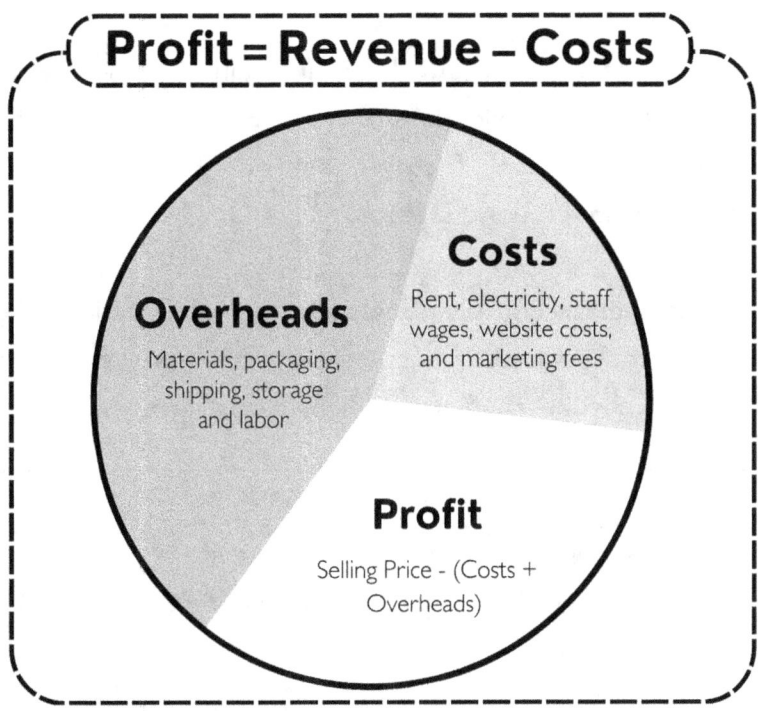

SETTING PRICES

Why can one hoodie cost $30 while another costs $75?

Sometimes it comes down to quality. The $75 hoodie might have better fabric, stitching, and durability. Often, it's less about the quality and more about **who made it, where it was made, and the name on the tag**.

Many companies use **cheap labor** in countries where workers are paid very little, which lowers costs. But pricing can also be influenced by the **"cool" factor** — people are often willing to pay more for popular brands and logos.

Bigger companies can also buy supplies and materials in bulk, resulting in cheaper prices. That means a hoodie from a large retailer will often be cheaper than one made by a small independent brand.

> **Challenge:** Imagine starting your own business. Choose a product you could make or a service you could offer. What would you need to charge your customers? What costs are involved? Thinking about these things can help you understand the real value of the stuff you buy.

Making Money

Did you know that some of today's jobs **didn't even exist** when your parents or grandparents started working? While there are still traditional careers like doctors, lawyers, and hotel managers, **new job opportunities** — like being a **YouTuber, app developer, or social media strategist** — are now part of the mix.

Making money **isn't just about** clocking in at 9 and out at 5 anymore. People earn money in all kinds of ways!

Traditional Jobs

These jobs have existed for years and often involve working for a company or in a specific role. Think teachers, factory workers, doctors, engineers, and lawyers.

- **Pros:** Traditional jobs offer a steady paycheck and often include benefits (paid holidays, health insurance, etc.).
- **Cons:** You work for someone else and don't have much flexibility in what you earn or the time you get off.

Freelancing

Freelancers are **independent workers for hire**. They provide services to companies or individuals but aren't full-time employees.

Many **graphic designers, writers, and social media managers** work this way.

- **Pros:** You have lots of flexibility, set your own rates and choose who to work with.
- **Cons:** You don't always earn a steady income and you have to find your own clients.

ENTREPRENEURSHIP

Entrepreneurship **sounds fancy**, but it just means **starting your own business**. You come up with an idea, create a product or service, and sell it. Some people **restore and sell vintage furniture, make handmade jewelry for Etsy, or start a garden service**.

- **Pros:** You get to be creative, set your schedule, and be your own boss.
- **Cons:** Starting a business is risky, and you're responsible for everything.

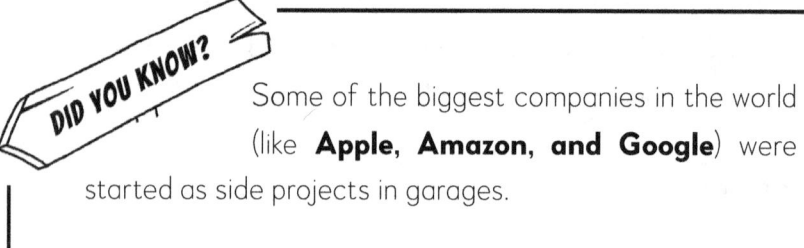

DID YOU KNOW? Some of the biggest companies in the world (like **Apple, Amazon, and Google**) were started as side projects in garages.

Investing

You can make money in other ways too — like **investing**. When you invest, you put your money toward something with the hope that it will **grow in value** over time.

Some people invest in **stocks** (owning a small piece of a company), while others buy **real estate** (property they rent out or use as a vacation rental).

- **Pros:** Your money grows without you actively working for it.
- **Cons:** It can be risky. Companies can lose money or go out of business, and all types of investments can lose value.

Figuring out what you want to do when you're older can feel overwhelming, and you don't need to figure it out now. But you can start noticing what the people around you do to make money.

Side Hustles

You may not be old enough to get a "real" job yet, but that doesn't mean you can't **make some money for yourself**. A side hustle is a way to earn money outside your main responsibilities (like school). Think of it as a small business or job you do in your free time to earn extra cash for things you want.

Online Side Hustle Ideas

- **Sell digital products** like art, planners, or calendars. You can create them using Procreate or Canva and list them on Etsy, Gumroad, Payhip, or Kofi.
- **Start a YouTube channel** or Patreon account (with your parents' permission). If you love Lego, cooking, gaming, crafts, or doing wacky experiments, chances are other people like the same thing or want to learn about it.

Offline Side Hustle Ideas

- If you like animals, you could try **pet-sitting or dog walking**. Put up flyers and tell your friends and family about your services.
- If you prefer kids to animals, **babysitting** might be for you. If you want to learn another cool life skill in the process, look into a CPR certification.
- If you're crafty, you can try **selling your creations at local markets** or to friends at school.

Side Hustle Pro Tips

- **Spread the word** — no one can buy your stuff or use your service if they haven't heard of it!
- **Set a fair price**, but don't sell yourself short.
- **Be reliable and responsible** and never put yourself in danger.

- **Keep learning** and find ways to improve your skills and business.

Digital vs. Physical Money

These days, most money exists in the digital world and never even touches your hands. Learning how to manage money can be tricky when you don't handle cash often because it almost doesn't feel real. But understanding both physical and digital money is important for being financially smart and responsible.

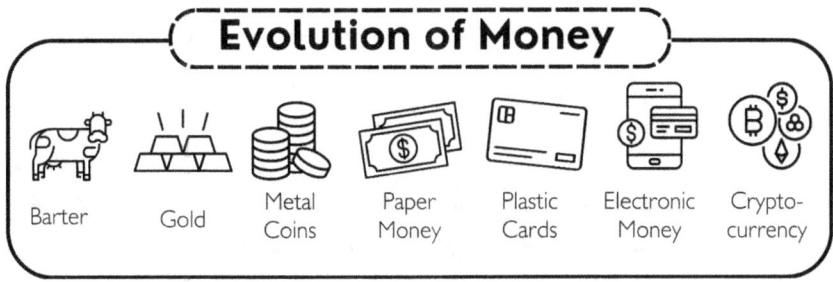

Physical Money

Some places don't accept card payments. That's why it's a good idea to **carry a little cash** just in case.

Understanding how to use physical cash is a critical life skill. When you have physical money in your wallet, **it's easier to see what you're spending** and what you have left. The downside is that physical money can get lost or stolen, so you need to look after it.

Tips to keep your physical money safe:

- Don't carry too much cash.
- Use a small wallet or pouch that fits snugly in your pocket.
- Don't leave your money lying around or let strangers see it.
- Be aware of your surroundings when you're withdrawing money at an ATM.

Digital Money

Do you have an **eWallet or online bank account**? Digital money is just as real as physical money, and it's a quick and convenient way to pay for things. Let's look at a few **digital payment methods**:

Online Banking

Online banking lets you manage your money using a **computer, tablet, or phone** instead of going to a bank. You can check your balance, pay bills, and transfer money easily.

Debit and Credit Cards

Both debit and credit cards are plastic (or digital) cards you can use to pay for things without needing cash. But they work differently.

- **Debit cards:** Think of your debit card as your wallet in card form. The transaction won't go through if there's no money in your account.

- **Credit cards:** A credit card is like **borrowing money** from the bank. You get a bill at the end of the month and have to pay it back — sometimes with extra fees and interest if you don't pay it all on time.

Mobile Payment Apps

Mobile payment apps are like having a digital wallet on your phone. Instead of pulling out cash or a card, you can tap, scan, or click on your phone to pay for stuff. Many payment apps exist, including **Apple Pay** (for iPhone users), **Google Wallet** (for Android users), **PayPal, Venmo, and CashApp**.

Cryptocurrency

Cryptocurrency is a type of money that only exists online. Instead of banks keeping track of who owns what, it's recorded on something called a blockchain. **Bitcoin** is the most well-known cryptocurrency, but crypto values **can change wildly** and be harder to secure than regular money.

How to Be Safe Using Digital Money

Where there is money, scammers will try to take it. Follow these tips to stay safe and keep your money secure.

DO:

- ☑ **Keep apps and devices updated** — this helps block security threats.
- ☑ **Use strong passwords** — mix letters, numbers, and symbols.
- ☑ **Change passwords regularly** — and don't reuse the same one for multiple accounts.
- ☑ **Turn on two-factor authentication** — this adds an extra layer of security.
- ☑ **Use screen locks** — like fingerprint or face unlock for your phone.
- ☑ **Check your transactions** — if you see **suspicious charges**, report them immediately.

DON'T:

- ☒ Never share your PIN, passwords, or account numbers — even with friends.
- ☒ If a stranger asks for your financial details, don't give them anything.
- ☒ Don't click links in emails or messages asking for personal info.
- ☒ Avoid using public Wi-Fi for banking or online purchases — it's not secure.

☒ Be cautious of "money-making" schemes — if it sounds too good to be true, it's probably a scam.

Being a Smart Shopper

Budgeting and knowing how to manage your money are great skills. But learning how to be a smart shopper can help you **get more for your money**. You're never too young to **shop smart**, so start using these tips today!

Compare Prices

Before you buy that t-shirt you've been eyeing, check out other stores and online marketplaces. You **may find it cheaper somewhere else** or even on sale online.

Know the Value

Just because the price tag says "50% off" doesn't mean it's a great deal — what if the item wasn't worth the full price in the first place? If a plain blue hoodie is priced at **$300** but marked down to **$100**. That might seem like a bargain — **until you realize you can get the same hoodie for $25 elsewhere.**

WAIT FOR SALES

If you're patient, you can wait for **Black Friday, Cyber Monday, or back-to-school sales**. Some online stores have an email list you can sign up to — you'll get an email when they have a sale.

SMART SHOPPING TIPS

- **Check reviews** before you spend money on something.
- **Don't buy things just because they're on sale**.
- If you're not 100% sure you want to buy something (and even if you are), **think about it for a few days**.

Understanding Money Matters

Money management is a life skill that puts you in control. Whether you're learning to save for your next big purchase, want to sharpen your deal-spotting skills, or thinking about creative side gigs, you need to understand money.

The more you learn and practice, the more confident you'll feel about handling money. And hey, even if you make a few mistakes along the way — that's all part of the journey. The important thing is to keep learning, think before you spend, and pay attention to your finances.

EMOTIONAL GROWTH AND SOCIAL SKILLS

You're at a stage in life where things might feel **new and exciting** — but also a little **scary**. Emotions can be **messy, overwhelming, confusing, and wonderful** all at once. As you head into your teen years, you might start looking at the world (and yourself) differently. Don't worry — **this is completely normal!**

This chapter is all about **emotional growth and social skills** — the things that help you **handle tough feelings, bounce back from failure, communicate better, and build strong relationships**.

Handling Big Emotions

Big emotions and changing moods can be confusing. Not only can they change quickly, but sometimes you might not understand why you feel a certain way.

Although they can be overwhelming, feelings aren't bad. **Emotions are just signals from your brain** that something is happening around you. While there are **no bad emotions, there can be bad reactions to emotions**. That's why learning to manage your feelings is important.

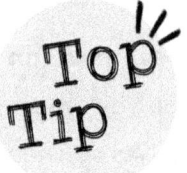

A Feelings Wheel can help you discover what you're really feeling. For example, you might think you're angry when, actually, you're embarrassed, frustrated, or irritated.

One of the biggest and trickiest emotions to deal with during your teen years is anger.

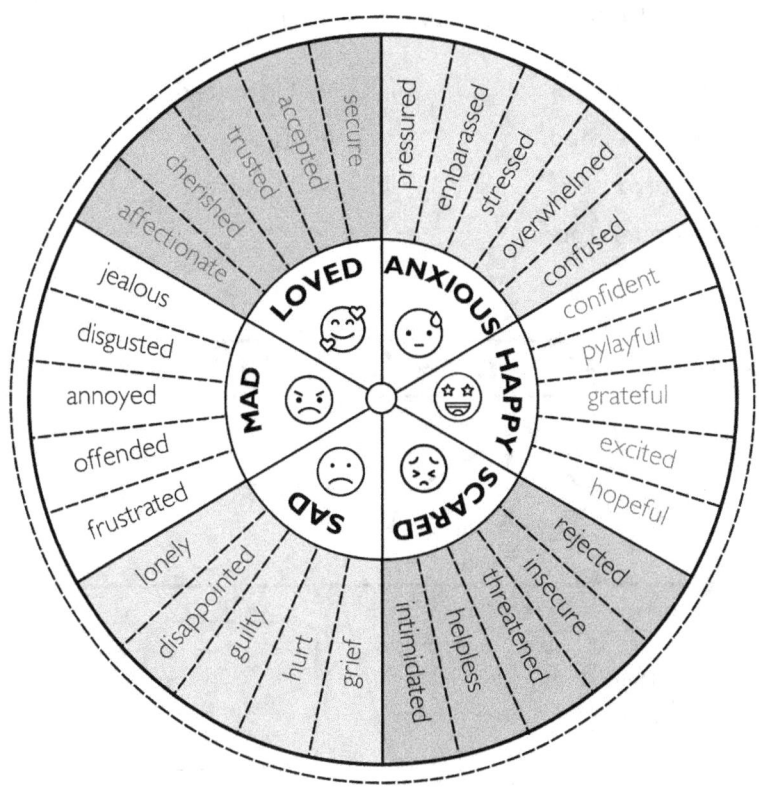

ANGER

Anger can be **explosive and make you feel out of control**. Don't worry, it's not just you — adults can feel that way too. The important thing is knowing how to stop your anger from taking over or causing you to hurt yourself or others. You have **more control than you think**, even if it doesn't feel like it. You just need a few strategies to help you in those heated moments.

But why do you get angry?

You're more likely to get angry if you feel:

- Stressed
- Overwhelmed
- Embarrassed
- Misunderstood
- Criticized
- Tired
- Hungry

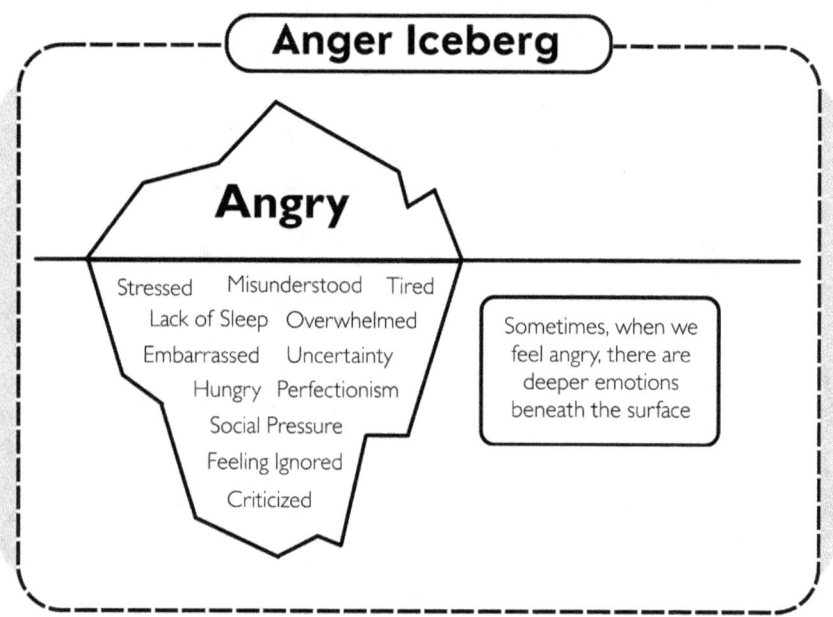

Did you know that your **brain is still developing** and **won't be fully developed until you're 25**? That means that the parts of your brain that control emotional responses are still learning what to do when they are faced with tricky situations and strong feelings.

When you're angry, you might notice **your heart racing, muscles clenching**, and **your breathing getting faster**. This is because anger sends your body into "**fight or flight**" mode. It's a survival mechanism to help you move quickly and get out of a dangerous situation, and it helped our prehistoric ancestors escape when they were being chased by terrifying creatures. Makes sense if you're faced with a bear, right? But not very helpful when solving conflicts with a friend or parent. Arguing with your friend isn't the same thing as being chased by a ravenous predator, and your body needs to learn how to tell the difference.

So, what can you do?

1. Identify Your Triggers

A trigger is something that "sets you off." It could be a **situation or topic** that immediately makes you angry. Knowing what makes you angry gives you more power and control.

- **Notice patterns:** Think back to times when you felt upset or overwhelmed. **What was happening? Who was there?** Write it down if it helps.
- **Pay attention to body signals:** Your body often knows you're triggered before your brain catches up. Do your fists clench? Does your face get hot? Does your heart race? Those are clues.

- **Ask yourself why:** When you feel triggered, pause and think: **"Why did that bother me so much?"** Sometimes, the reason isn't obvious at first, but it's worth exploring.

Anger Triggers

An anger trigger is something that makes you feel annoyed, frustrated, or angry. Read each item and rank from 1-10 how angry each trigger makes you.

```
0   1   2   3   4   5   6   7   8   9   10
Calm     Annoyed     Irritated     Angry     Furious
```

- ☐ Being blamed for something I didn't do.
- ☐ Hearing unfair comparisons to siblings or other kids.
- ☐ Watching my things get taken without permission.
- ☐ Dealing with broken promises.
- ☐ Struggling with a tough test and ending up with a bad grade.
- ☐ Getting left out of plans or group activities.
- ☐ Messing up in a game and hearing people make fun of me.
- ☐ Feeling pressured to do something I don't want to do.
- ☐ Losing privileges or getting grounded for something small.
- ☐ Being rushed to finish something when I need more time.

---

2. Talk It Out

Once you've cooled down, think about what made you mad, and then chat about it. Your sibling might have violated your personal space by entering your room without knocking. But if they don't know it's a problem for you, they'll keep doing it. Make sure to **calmly explain why certain things make you angry.**

3. Breathe

Breathing techniques help take your body out of "fight or flight" mode and get back to normal. **Andrew Huberman**, a neuroscientist, has a quick breathing technique to help calm you down during a tense moment. He calls it a **"psychological sigh."** It goes like this:

- **Two short inhales through the nose.**
- **One long exhale through the mouth.**
- **Repeat three times.**

What NOT to Do:

- ☒ **Lash out** by yelling or hitting.
- ☒ **Bottle up your anger** and ignore it.
- ☒ **Blame yourself** for feeling mad — anger is normal!

Resilience

Life doesn't always go as planned. Maybe you flunked a quiz or didn't make the team. That's where resilience comes in — it's about **being able to bounce back** when you experience a setback.

Did you know that every successful person you admire has faced failure and rejection? What sets them apart is the ability to bounce back, learn, and move forward.

DID YOU KNOW? Bethany Hamilton is a professional surfer who lost her arm in a shark attack when she was 13. One month later, she was back in the water, and two years later, she won first place in the Explorer Women's Division of the NSSA National Championships. That's resilience in action!

Growth Mindset

Learning to be resilient comes from having a **growth mindset**. You've probably heard the phrase, "*Practice makes perfect.*" Well, a growth mindset changes that by saying, **"*Practice makes progress.*"**

Having a growth mindset means you see your mistakes as **opportunities to learn** — you know that your abilities and intelligence will improve with effort and perseverance.

On the flip side, a **fixed mindset** is when you believe that your abilities are set in stone. If you're bad at something, you think you'll always be bad at it.

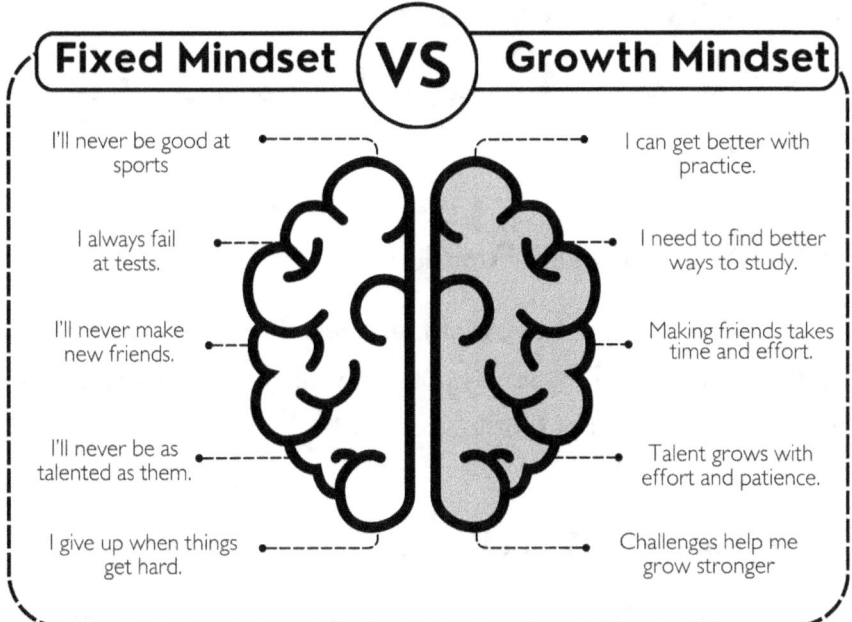

Let's look at some examples:

Fixed mindset: "*I'm just bad at writing.*"

Growth mindset: "*I didn't do well on this essay, but I can get better by practicing.*"

Fixed mindset: "*I can't draw. I'm not artistic.*"

Growth mindset: "*I don't know how to draw yet, but I can learn by following tutorials.*"

Tips for Building Resilience

You can work on your resilience just like any other skill. These tips will help.

Talk to Yourself Like a Friend

If your friend had flunked a math test, would you say, "*Wow, you're really bad at math*"? Hopefully not — it would be cruel and rude! So why would you talk like that to yourself?

Learn From What Went Wrong

Getting things wrong isn't a problem. If something goes wrong, you now know what *doesn't* work and you can try something different. Sometimes, **you have to get something wrong before you get it right** — like practicing a skateboard trick.

Take a Break

It's normal to feel disappointed when things don't go your way, and it's okay to take a break. But that doesn't mean you should stop trying. A break gives you space to feel your feelings and come up with a new strategy, or think about something else for a while. You'll come back to the problem refreshed and ready to go!

Use the Power of "Yet"

That tiny word — **yet** — changes everything. For example, instead of "*I can't do this,*" try "*I can't do this **yet**.*" It tells your brain, "*This is hard now, but with time and effort, I'll get better.*"

Keep trying, even when it's frustrating. **Struggle doesn't mean failure — it means you're growing.**

All About You: Self-Esteem, Self-Compassion, and Self-Awareness

Self-esteem, self-compassion, and self-awareness are all about **how you see and treat yourself**. They are interconnected but focus on different things.

Self-Esteem: How You Feel About Yourself

Self-esteem is your overall sense of self-worth — whether you believe you're valuable, capable, and deserving of respect.

When you have healthy self-esteem, you:

- Trust yourself.
- Feel good about who you are.
- Aren't afraid to make mistakes.

When you have low self-esteem, you:

- Doubt yourself.
- Feel like you're not good enough.
- Compare yourself to others.

Example: Say you mess up on a school project. If you have **healthy self-esteem**, you think, *"That didn't go so well, but I can do better* next time." **Low self-esteem** might make you think, *"I'm so dumb. I'll never be good at this."* Guess which mindset is more helpful?

Self Esteem Journal

Try recording your thoughts and feelings to help you **understand and improve** your self-esteem. Use this worksheet to get started, or write in a notebook. Use words, pictures, or anything else that helps you express your feelings.

Self-Esteem Journal

Something good that happened to me today was:

Something positive someone said about me:

A compliment that I would give myself today is:

Positive feelings that I experienced today:

I made someone else feel good when I:

I had a negative thought about myself when:

Self-Awareness: Understanding Your Thoughts, Feelings, and Actions

Being self-aware means you can **recognize your emotions, habits, and reactions**. It helps you understand why you feel or act a certain way so you can make better choices.

Self-awareness helps you **respond**, rather than **react**. A response is intentional and controlled, whereas a reaction is based on emotion — something you do without thinking.

These are the three R's of responsiveness:

- **Recognize:** Identify what triggered you.
- **Regulate:** Take a few deep breaths to calm yourself, and take your body out of fight or flight mode.
- **Reflect:** Think about what happened and how you could handle the situation differently.

Example: You snap at a friend because you're tired and stressed. If you have self-awareness, you realize, *"I was rude because I had a bad day. I should apologize."* Without self-awareness, you might not even notice how your mood affects your behavior.

Mood Tracker

Make a copy of this simple tracker and fill it out to understand how your moods change from day to day.

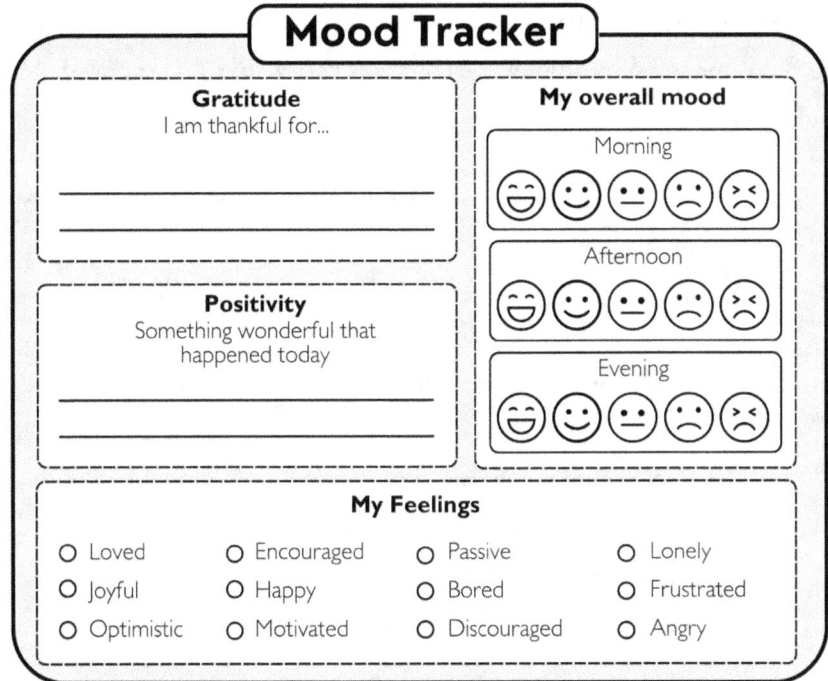

SELF-COMPASSION: BEING KIND TO YOURSELF

Self-compassion means **treating yourself** with the same **kindness** you would show a friend. Everyone messes up, faces hard times, or falls short of their own expectations sometimes. How you treat yourself during those tough times is important.

Self-compassion is crucial because talking badly about yourself only makes you feel worse. If your inner voice is always critical, it can be really hard to try new things or learn from your mistakes.

Example: You fail a test. Instead of saying, *"I'm so stupid,"* you show self-compassion by thinking, *"That was tough, but I'll prepare better next time."*

DID YOU KNOW?

Self-esteem, self-compassion, and self-awareness work together:

- **Self-awareness** helps you notice when you're being too hard on yourself.
- **Self-compassion** helps you be gentle and encouraging instead of critical.
- **Self-esteem** grows stronger when you recognize your worth, even when things don't go perfectly.

Stress Management

The teen years can be stressful. You're going through a lot of **changes**, both **physical and emotional**. Life can feel like a lot!

You might be juggling friendships, sports, extra-curriculars, academics, and navigating the changing dynamic with your parents. You may also start looking at the world differently and wondering who you are and where you fit in. It's all normal! But that doesn't mean that the pressure isn't stressful to deal with.

If you're stressed, you might:

- Feel really tired.
- Get stomach aches.
- Struggle to focus.
- Put things off or try to avoid them.
- Feel angry or upset.
- Withdraw from friends and family.

Stress activates your "fight or flight" response and can heighten your emotions (like anger). One of the best ways to deal with stress is to activate your **parasympathetic nervous system (PNS)**. The PNS is a network of nerves that helps **relax your body**. When you activate the PNS, you turn off the "flight or fight" response and activate the "rest and digest" response.

DID YOU KNOW? The sympathetic nervous system (fight or flight) carries signals that put your body on high alert. The parasympathetic nervous system (rest and digest) carries signals that put your body back in balance.

HANDLING STRESS

Here are some strategies you can use to calm yourself down when you're stressed.

Mindfulness and Gratitude

Are you stressing about something that hasn't happened yet? Instead of worrying about the future, **focus on the present**. Notice the things around you. **What can you hear, see, smell, taste, and feel**? Breathe deeply and **stay in the moment**. Grounding yourself in the present moment and being thankful can help you reframe the situation and feel less stressed.

Gratitude can help you to appreciate what you have rather than worrying about what you don't have. To practice gratitude, **try writing down three things you are grateful for every day**. Noticing what you have instead of focusing on what you don't can help you feel less anxious.

Sleep

Not getting enough sleep makes everything harder and can make emotions feel stronger and less predictable. Being tired means more stress, mood swings, brain fog, and bad decision-making! **Most people need around 8–10 hours of sleep a night**. How many hours do *you* get?

Tips for getting a good night's sleep:

- **Turn off screens** (phone, tablet, TV...) at least 30 minutes before bed.
- **Stick to a bedtime routine** that tells your brain it's time for sleep.
- **Go to sleep and wake up at the same time** every day (even on weekends).

Relaxation Techniques

Relaxation techniques are simple ways to calm your mind and body when life feels overwhelming and stressful. When you're stressed, your nervous system kicks into "fight-or-flight" mode. Relaxation techniques can send your brain the signal that you're safe, helping you get back to normal.

You can use these techniques anytime — before a test, after an argument, when you're having trouble sleeping, or even just to recharge after a long day.

4-7-8 Breathing

1. Inhale through your nose for four seconds.
2. Hold your breath for seven seconds.
3. Exhale slowly for eight seconds.

Muscle Relaxation

1. Tighten a part of your body (like your fists or shoulders) for five seconds.
2. Release and feel the tension fade.
3. Work your way through your body.

Visualization

1. Close your eyes and imagine a place where you feel calm — maybe the beach, your room, or a cozy forest.
2. Picture every detail, like sounds, colors, and smells.
3. You can also listen to a guided visualization.

SCHOOL PRESSURE

Stress can help you do your best at school, but it can also make school feel overwhelming. Homework, tests, sports, friends, and parental expectations are a lot to deal with. If you're struggling to handle everything, **talk to your parents and teachers**. Reaching out for support shows strength, not weakness.

Here are a few more things you can try to make school less stressful.

Break Big Tasks Into Smaller Ones

Looking at a huge project as one big task can make it feel impossible. Instead, **break it down into bite-sized steps and tackle one at a time**. This also helps you plan your time better.

Make a Study Schedule

Studying feels way less overwhelming when you have a plan. Cramming everything in at the last minute can make you feel frazzled and stressed. **Breaking tasks into smaller, manageable chunks** and spreading them out over time can help you focus and get things done.

Start by writing down what you need to do. Then, decide when you'll do each task. It's important to be realistic, so don't schedule too much in one day. When you're done, cross the task off the list. Seeing your completed tasks can help keep you motivated.

Use the Pomodoro Technique

Using this method can help you be productive without feeling burnt out or overwhelmed. It's simple:

1. Study for 25 minutes.
2. Take a five-minute break.
3. Repeat a few times, then take a longer break.

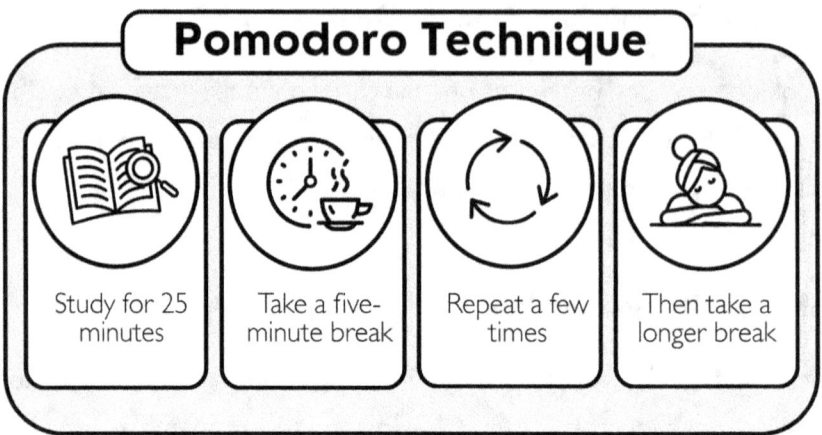

Don't Be Afraid to Say "No"

If your schedule is packed, it's okay to cut back on extracurricular activities or skip that weekend hangout to catch up on rest.

Avoid last-minute cramming. Studying a little each day works better.

Your brain works better when it's rested, so get those ZZZ's.

Put things into perspective. One test doesn't define your entire future, no matter how it feels in the moment.

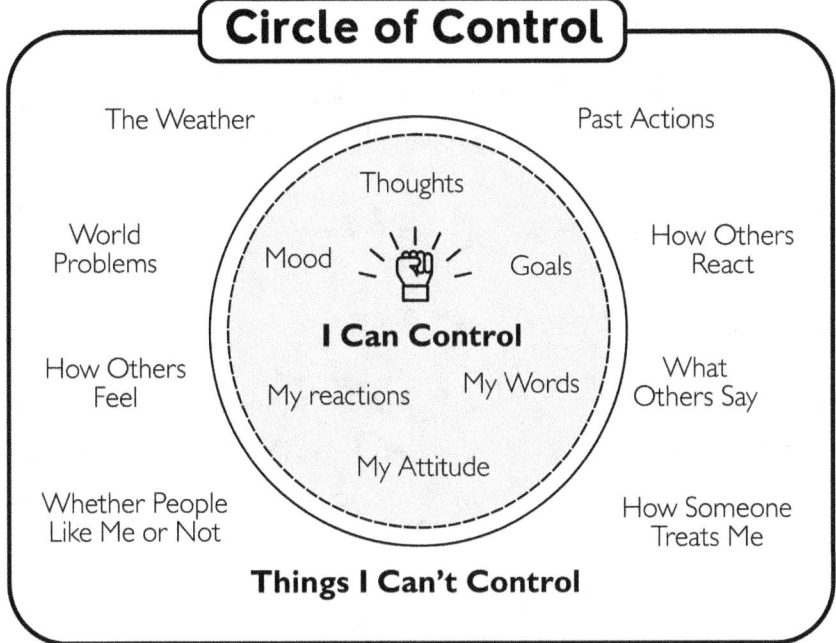

STRESS VS. ANXIETY

Anxiety and stress feel similar, but they're not the same. Both can make your heart race, your stomach hurt, and your brain feel overwhelmed, but stress is usually caused by something specific, while anxiety can strike even when there's no clear reason for it.

Stress

Stress happens when you're dealing with a tough situation like a big test, a sports competition, or too many responsibilities at once. It's your body's way of preparing to handle a challenge, and it often goes away once the stressful event is over.

Signs of stress:

- Feeling overwhelmed, but knowing why.
- Physical symptoms like headaches or tense muscles.
- Difficulty getting to sleep.
- The feeling goes away once the stressful event is over.

Anxiety

Anxiety is more than stress. **It can be a constant worry that doesn't always have a clear cause**. Even after the stressful event is over, anxiety can stick around, making you feel restless or scared for no reason.

Signs of anxiety:

- Worrying even when nothing is wrong.
- Difficulty relaxing or focusing.
- Physical symptoms like nausea or trouble sleeping.
- The feeling comes and goes for no obvious reason.

Stress and anxiety are normal sometimes, but if they are starting to interfere with your life, **ask for help**.

Communication and Listening Skills

Ever had a conversation where you felt like the other person wasn't really listening? Maybe they were on their phone, interrupting, or just waiting for their turn to talk. Annoying, right? But here's the thing — *we all do that sometimes.*

Good communication isn't just about talking. **It's about listening, understanding, and responding** in a way that makes the other person feel **heard and valued**. Good communication can help you build stronger friendships and avoid misunderstandings. It's also extremely helpful as you learn to relate to your parents in a new way.

LEARNING TO LISTEN

A major part of communication is learning how to listen.

Actually Pay Attention

It's easy to get distracted when you're chatting with someone. But being fully engaged in the conversation shows that you're interested in what they have to say and how they feel.

- If you have a phone, **put it away**.
- **Make eye contact** (but don't go overboard and make it weird — see below.)

- **Focus on what they're saying** instead of thinking about what you're going to say.
- **Don't interrupt**.

Make Eye Contact

Look at the person when they're talking, but don't stare them down. A rule says you should make eye contact for 70% of the conversation in four- to five-second bursts. If eye contact feels awkward, try looking at the space between their eyebrows.

Ask Good Questions

People love to talk about themselves, so asking questions is an easy way to be more engaged in a conversation and make the other person feel valued.

Try:

- How did that make you feel?
- What happened next?
- Can you tell me more?

Silence can also be powerful. If someone has shared something vulnerable with you, silence can make space for their feelings. **Don't always feel you need to say something.**

Communicating So People Listen

Do you ever feel like you're talking, but no one is listening? Or does the idea of talking to new people freak you out because what you say never quite comes out right? Good communication is all about what you say and how you say it. When you speak clearly and with confidence, people are more likely to listen, understand, and respect what you have to say.

Be Clear and Direct

If you're upset, instead of saying, *"You never listen to me!"* try, *"I feel ignored when you're on your phone while I'm talking."* **People respond better when they know exactly what's wrong.**

Use "I" Statements Instead of Blame

Saying, *"You always interrupt me!"* can make someone defensive. Instead, try *"I feel frustrated when I get interrupted because I really want to finish my thought."* **"I" statements don't blame or accuse the other person.**

Watch Your Tone and Body Language

Saying *"I'm fine"* with crossed arms and an eye roll sends a different message (more on this in the next chapter) than saying it calmly.

Your facial expressions, posture, and tone can say as much as your words.

Know When to Pause

If you're feeling angry or upset, **take a breath** before responding. A simple *"Can we talk about this later?"* can prevent an argument from escalating or you saying something you'll regret.

Match the Method to the Message

Some conversations are better in person than over text, messenger, or email. If the topic is serious, like apologizing or discussing feelings, **talk face-to-face** instead of sending a message that could be misunderstood.

Emotions Are Awesome

Learning to manage your feelings, handle stress, and communicate with confidence isn't about being perfect. What matters is that you **keep learning** — whether that's bouncing back from a bad day, standing up for yourself, or showing kindness when someone else is struggling. You won't always get it right, and that's okay. **The more you practice, the better you'll get** at handling whatever life throws your way.

NAVIGATING THE SOCIAL WORLD

As you get older, you might notice **your world is changing**. You may be exploring new interests, making new friends, and testing your boundaries. Your teenage years are for learning about who you are, taking on more responsibility, and becoming more independent. It's an exhilarating time full of experiences — some awesome, some... not so much.

Sometimes, it might feel like you're wading through muddy water as you try to navigate friendships, fights, and your changing body image. Although it can feel overwhelming, a few helpful hints and tips can go a long way! This chapter will give you the scoop on reading **body language, handling conflict, and setting boundaries**. It will also **explain peer pressure** and help you **identify gaslighting**.

Reading the Room

Every situation has unspoken social cues and rules. If you've ever made a loud entrance into a quiet room...you get it! Social cues are signals that help you figure out what's going on and how to respond. "Reading the room" is a skill that will help you **assess situations quickly** and decide how best to act.

Understanding Social Cues

Social cues are things like **body language, tone of voice, facial expressions, and even clothing**. They can tell you if a conversation is serious or casual and give you a hint about whether it's a good time for you to join in or not.

Every setting has "rules," like being quiet in a library or not using your phone in a movie theater. Social cues help you adapt your behavior to suit the "rules" of the situation.

Here are some tips for reading the room:

- **Observe first.** Before interrupting a conversation, take a moment to **assess the situation**. What is the "vibe"? Would your interruption be welcome? If not, save it for later.
- **Match the mood.** Laughing and telling jokes isn't appropriate in the library, but it is totally okay at your local pizza place. If you're not sure, watch what other people are doing.

- **Pay attention to people's reactions.** Are they confused, annoyed, uninterested, or happy? Their reactions will tell you if you read the room correctly. Don't worry if you get it wrong; just save that information for next time.

Understanding social cues isn't about changing who you are to fit in. It's about knowing how to connect with people in the moment. It takes time to learn the "rules," and everyone gets it wrong sometimes, so don't stress if you find people and situations confusing!

Micro-Expressions and Body Language

The quickest way to read the room is to notice people's body language and micro-expressions. These are the things people say without words.

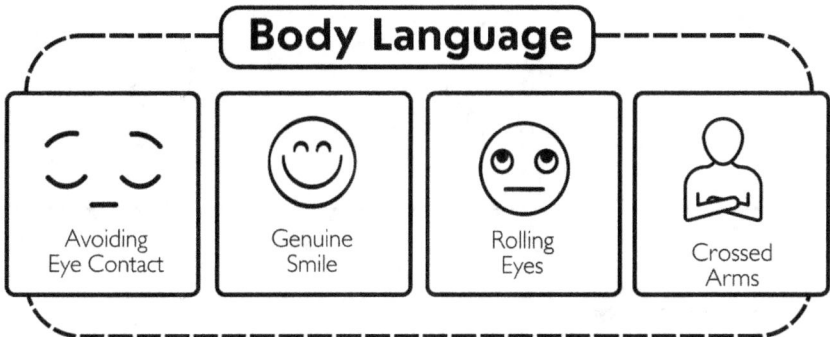

Body Language

Your body can send signals whether you mean it to or not. Here are some common body language signals:

- **Leaning in:** Interested, engaged.
- **Crossed arms:** Defensive, unsure, closed off, uncomfortable.
- **Making eye contact:** Engaged, interested, listening.
- **Avoiding eye contact:** Nervous, shy, hiding something.
- **Fidgeting:** Anxious, impatient.
- **Relaxed hands:** Calm, confident.
- **Facing away:** Uncomfortable, bored.
- **Genuine smile:** Warm, approachable.
- **Rolling eyes:** Dismissive, irritated.

Context matters! Someone might be crossing their arms because they're upset, or they might just be cold. Don't jump to conclusions with body language — it's more like a clue to how someone is feeling than a manual!

Micro-Expressions

Have you ever said you were fine but were hurt or angry? Your face probably gave you away without you even realizing it. The tiny changes in your face and body often tell other people how you're really feeling.

Here are some examples of micro-expressions:

- **Anger:** Lips pressed together, flaring nostrils.
- **Surprise:** Raised eyebrows, wide eyes, open mouth.
- **Fear:** Eyebrows raised and drawn together, eyes wide.
- **Sadness:** Lowered eyes, frown, downturned mouth.
- **Happiness:** A real smile that causes crinkles at the corner of the eyes.
- **Disgust:** Upper lip is raised, nose is wrinkled.

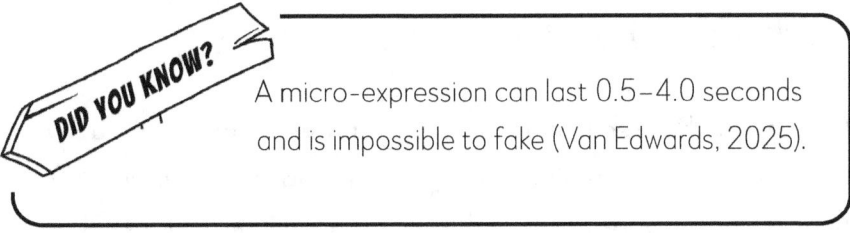

DID YOU KNOW? A micro-expression can last 0.5–4.0 seconds and is impossible to fake (Van Edwards, 2025).

Handling Conflict

Conflict is a part of life, no matter how much you try to avoid it. It could be anything from **fighting with your parents** about a curfew to arguing with a classmate during a group project. There's nothing wrong with some healthy conflict occasionally — **you won't get along with everyone all the time**, and that's alright. But knowing how to handle conflict can make a big difference. It's important to learn **how to handle conflict** in a way that you can feel proud of.

MISUNDERSTANDINGS

Many conflicts happen because of misunderstandings. With misunderstandings, the clue is in the name — they happen when people don't understand each other correctly. Misunderstandings can lead to all kinds of trouble if not cleared up quickly!

Here's an example:

You ask your friend in class if they want to hang out this weekend. They say they'll check and let you know, but by Friday, you still haven't heard back. You start thinking, *"Maybe they don't want to hang out... Maybe they're mad at me!"* So, you mention it to another friend, wondering what you did wrong.

But here's what really happened — your friend got caught up with family plans and completely forgot to get back to you. When they hear that you were upset and talking about it with someone else, they feel hurt because they weren't ignoring you on purpose.

Misunderstandings happen all the time, but there are a few ways you can help prevent them:

- **Ask, don't assume.** Instead of jumping to, *"They must be mad at me,"* reach out and ask, *"Hey, are we okay?"*
- **Listen first.** Let the other person explain before jumping in. If you start making accusations without hearing the whole story, it will make the situation worse.

- **Apologize if necessary.** If you were wrong, say sorry!

Dealing With Difficult People

Not everyone is easy to get along with. Everyone has their own quirks, struggles, and insecurities — some people are bossy, some are negative, and some just rub you the wrong way. **You'll come across difficult people at all stages of life**, and you need to know how to handle them. These tips will help.

Pick Your Battles

Sometimes, it's better to **ignore someone or leave a situation** that isn't worth your time and energy. Think carefully about what staying in the situation will achieve.

Set Boundaries

If someone keeps treating you badly, **limit the time you spend with them**. You can explain that as long as they are bossy or negative (or whatever it is), they won't get to be around you.

Stay Respectful

Be the bigger person and **speak calmly and respectfully**. Getting angry and confrontational will only make the situation worse.

Look At Yourself

Sometimes, people bring out the worst in each other. Do you ever do or say things that trigger someone to be difficult? For example, saying, "*You always...*" or "*You never...*" can make people feel like they need to defend themselves. **Think about how your words and actions affect people.** You might not be the problem, but they might not be either.

Bullies

Bullying is when someone repeatedly hurts, threatens, or embarrasses another person on purpose. It's not just about physical harm — bullying can also be **words, actions, or even online messages** meant to make someone feel small. It can happen anywhere — at school, in a group of friends, on social media, or at home.

There is no simple solution for dealing with bullying. It's a difficult situation that can make you feel vulnerable, scared, and angry. It can make you doubt yourself or feel like you don't belong. Sometimes, people who get bullied start avoiding places they used to enjoy or feel anxious all the time. **Bullying is never okay, and it's not your fault.** No one deserves to be treated that way.

Bullies thrive on making other people feel powerless, but you have more control than you think.

Stay Cool

Bullies want a reaction, so don't give it to them. They often want attention or the feeling of power when they hurt someone else. If they see that their actions upset you, they may feel like they "won" and keep doing it.

That's why one common strategy for dealing with bullies is to stay calm and not give them the reaction they're hoping for. **If you don't get upset or fight back, they might get bored and move on.**

Don't Engage Online

You can block and report if someone is bullying you online or over text messages. Before blocking them, **take screenshots** of any mean messages or posts. If things get worse, you'll have proof to show a trusted adult.

Tell an Adult

Bullying can feel overwhelming, but having support makes a big difference. **Telling a trusted adult** that you're being bullied is one of the smartest things you can do. Adults have experience and can give advice or step in if needed.

Don't Blame Yourself

Bullying is **never** your fault. No one deserves to be treated badly, no matter what. Bullies choose to act that way — that's on them, not you. It's easy to wonder if you did something wrong, but people bully for their own reasons.

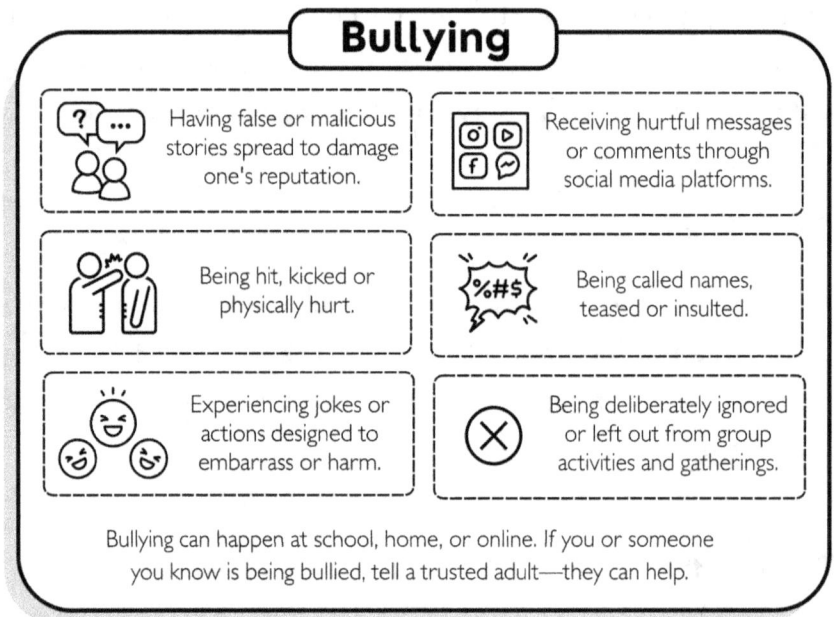

How to Apologize

Nobody likes to be wrong, but everyone makes mistakes sometimes. Maybe you forgot your friend's birthday or said something you didn't mean. **Mistakes are normal, but how you handle them matters.**

A real apology isn't just saying *"sorry."* When you apologize and mean it, you:

- **Take responsibility** for your actions.
- **Repair** the relationship.
- **Rebuild** trust.
- **Move forward.**

Five Steps for Good Apologies

Apologizing can be difficult because it means admitting you made a mistake. You might feel embarrassed, defensive, or angry at yourself. Here are some steps to make saying sorry a bit easier.

Step One: Own It

Saying something like, *"I'm sorry you feel that way"* or *"I guess I messed up"* doesn't send the message that you're *actually* sorry. These are weak apologies that could just make the situation worse.

Instead, **be clear about what you're apologizing for**. For example, *"I shouldn't have borrowed your hoodie without asking."* When you say sorry about specific actions, it shows maturity and makes your apology more meaningful.

Step Two: Don't Make Excuses

You might want to explain why you did what you did. But when you do, it sounds like you are trying to justify your actions rather than being sorry for them.

For example, *"I'm in a bad mood, that's why I snapped at you"* isn't an apology. But *"I shouldn't have snapped at you, I'm sorry"* is.

You also want to **avoid using the word "but."** Anything that comes after a "but" cancels out your apology!

Step Three: Make It Right

Sometimes words aren't enough, and you need to show how sorry you are. If your actions have affected someone negatively, think about ways to **fix it and repair trust**.

- If you broke or lost something, replace it.
- If you spread a rumor, correct it.
- If you hurt someone, ask how you can make it up to them.

Step Four: Learn From It

A great apology should include a plan to **do better next time**. If you keep making the same mistake, "sorry" loses its meaning.

Step Five: Give Them Space

Even if you've sincerely apologized, the person might need some space. Don't pressure them. Let them process their feelings and your apology in their own time.

Boundaries

A boundary is a clear limit you set to protect your time, energy, and well-being. Boundaries aren't about pushing people away. They are invisible lines you draw to protect your personal space and mental health.

A boundary is:

- **Saying no** when a friend pressures you to do something you don't want to.
- Telling a sibling that you need quiet time to focus on your homework.
- Asking someone not to make jokes at your expense.

A boundary isn't:

- Controlling what others do.
- Ignoring people just because you're mad.
- A command telling people what they can or can't do.

Boundaries help you to feel **safe and respected**. Sometimes, your gut might tell you someone is crossing a line that makes you uncomfortable. That's why setting boundaries isn't mean — it's healthy. They show people how to treat you, and good friends will respect them.

Setting boundaries can feel awkward, especially if you don't want to disappoint someone. But learning to say "no" confidently and without guilt is a valuable life skill.

Before you create a boundary, ask yourself: **What is the goal of this boundary?**

Do you want to protect your feelings, create healthier friendships, or balance your time? It's easier to enforce a boundary when you understand why it's important to you.

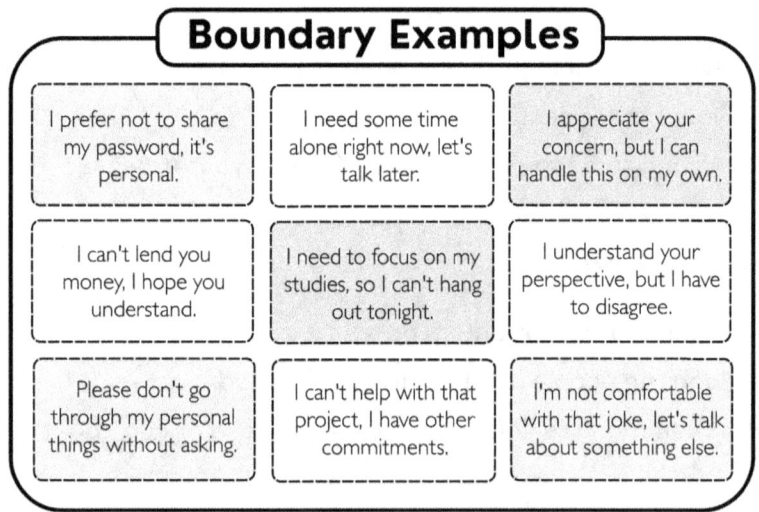

SETTING BOUNDARIES

Setting boundaries isn't about controlling other people or getting your way all the time. It's about creating a **healthy space for yourself while respecting others**. When you set a boundary, you're showing that you value yourself, but that doesn't mean you get to ignore other people's needs or feelings.

For example, setting a boundary like "*I need some time alone*" is great for your well-being, but it's also important to communicate that respectfully. Telling someone, "*I love hanging out with you, but I need some time to recharge right now,*" is better than shutting them down.

Also, be ready for some **compromise**. In a healthy relationship, boundaries can be somewhat negotiable. For example, if a friend asks for your help with something, you can say, "*I can help, but I need to finish my homework first.*" That way, you ask them to respect your boundaries while still helping out.

SAYING "NO" WITHOUT THE GUILT

Boundaries help you feel more in control of your life and relationships, but they can be difficult for others to accept. Sometimes, you'll need to enforce your boundaries. Here are some tips to help you feel more confident.

- **Offer an alternative** if you can. For example, if you want to study instead of meeting your friends for pizza, ask them for a rain check (and make sure to follow through.)
- **Be firm but kind** when you say no. For example, "*I appreciate you asking, but I can't today*," or "*I can't take that on right now.*"
- **You don't always need to give a long explanation.** "*No*" is a full sentence, and you don't need to justify your boundaries to someone who doesn't respect them.

Dealing With Pushback

Some people won't like or respect your boundaries, especially if they're used to you saying "*yes.*" **Stay firm**, and **don't feel pressured** to change your mind.

- If someone keeps trying to cross your boundary, **repeat it confidently**. You could say something like, "*I'm not comfortable with that. Please respect my decision.*"
- You don't owe anyone an explanation, but sometimes a short reason can help. For example, "*I can't let you copy my homework because I worked hard on it, and it wouldn't be fair.*"
- Sometimes people won't take no for an answer. Keep repeating your boundary without changing it. For example, "*I understand you want me to come, but I already said I need a break today.*"

Your boundaries aren't about saying *"I'm right and you're wrong."* They're about telling people what you need to feel good about yourself and respected by others.

ENDING RELATIONSHIPS AND FRIENDSHIPS

Not every friendship or relationship is meant to last. **People grow, change, and sometimes drift apart** — it's a part of life. Relationships end naturally for all kinds of reasons, but sometimes you might need to end a relationship yourself, perhaps because it is unhealthy or makes you unhappy.

Here are some signs it might be time to move on from a friendship:

- It makes you feel **drained, upset, or stressed**.
- The person **doesn't respect your boundaries**, ignores your feelings, and breaks your trust.
- The friendship is **one-sided**, and you're often the one who makes plans, checks in, or offers support.
- The person brings out the worst in you or **encourages bad habits**.
- Your **values and priorities** have shifted.

Ending relationships and friendships is difficult, but you can **do it with respect and kindness**. Have an honest conversation and clearly explain why you want to end the friendship. You can also slowly start putting distance between you and the other person. The friendship may have already started to fade naturally as you focus on other friendships and activities.

If you find yourself in a toxic and unhealthy relationship, you should cut ties completely. Here are some signs that a relationship may have become toxic:

- They **don't respect your boundaries**.
- **You feel drained** or anxious around them.
- They make everything about them.
- They guilt-trip or **manipulate you**.
- They **embarrass you** or put you down.
- They **don't take responsibility** for their actions.
- You feel like you "owe" them your time and attention.

Don't stay in a relationship that makes you feel unsafe. If the other person isn't respecting your decision, talk with an adult about what to do.

Puberty and Body Image

Changing relationships aren't the only thing you'll experience as you grow older. Your body will also change.

Body image is how you see yourself and how you feel about your body. Society often encourages us to believe that we need to look a certain way to be "good enough." But bodies come in all shapes and sizes and one type isn't better than another.

When you have a **healthy body image**, you:

- **Appreciate what your body can do**, not just how it looks. You can stretch, dance, think, create, love, and so much more!
- **Don't have unrealistic beauty standards**. The images of people you see on social media, TV, or in magazines have usually been edited, filtered, or completely invented. No one looks "perfect" all the time.

Your body is changing and growing as it should! Instead of stressing over what you think it should look like, **focus on treating it with love, healthy food, rest, and movement.**

Your appearance is the least interesting thing about you. Your personality, talents, kindness, and passions matter way more than how you look.

Comparison Culture

It's easy to look around or on social media and think everyone else is cooler, more attractive, happier, or...whatever!

But are they really? No!

When you think of everyone else as being "better," it makes you feel like you're not good enough. **Comparing yourself with others can crush your joy**, making it harder to appreciate the qualities that make you unique. Choose your influences (and influencers!) wisely. Look to people who focus on confidence, self-love, and realness instead of putting on a show that makes you feel bad about yourself.

The only person you should compare yourself to is...YOU. Are you learning and growing? Are you becoming a better version of yourself? Life isn't a race or a competition. It's about learning to love who you are as you navigate the world around you.

Peer Pressure, Gaslighting, and Manipulation

Sometimes, people try to push you into doing things you don't want to do. It might be something obvious, like pressuring you into skipping class, or something more subtle, like trying to make you feel guilty for setting a boundary. Understanding peer pressure, gaslighting, and manipulation can help you recognize when something is off and stand up for yourself.

Peer Pressure

Peer pressure happens when people encourage or pressure you to do something. It could be something good (like trying a new hobby) or bad (like breaking a rule on purpose). Whenever people are trying to get you to do something, that's peer pressure. It's important to take a moment to think in these situations — **do things because you want to**, not because other people want you to.

The best way to handle peer pressure is to:

- **Trust your gut**. If it feels wrong then it probably is.
- **Have a firm go-to response** like, *"That's not for me. Stop pressuring me."*
- **Surround yourself with friends** who respect your boundaries.

Gaslighting

Gaslighting is when someone twists the truth to make you question your own memory or feelings. This is a common tactic in toxic friendships or relationships.

Gaslighting might look like:

- Saying things like, **"That never happened"** when you clearly remember something happening, or **"You're overreacting"** when you're upset or annoyed.
- **Trying to make you feel guilty** for standing up for yourself.
- **Changing the story** so they look like the victim.

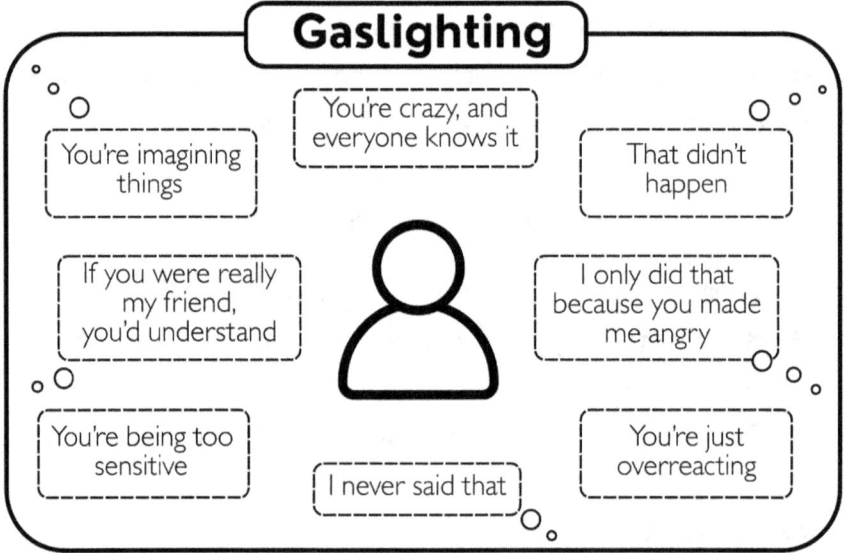

If someone often makes you question your reality, take a step back and talk to a trusted friend or adult for an outside perspective.

MANIPULATION

Manipulation is when someone tries to control you or your decisions by guilt-tripping, lying, or twisting the truth. It's sneaky because the person usually makes it seem like they're doing it for your own good.

Manipulation red flags:

- **Guilt trips** like saying, "*If you were really my friend, you'd do this.*"
- **Refusing to speak to you** until you give them what they want.
- **Faking kindness to get what they want**. For example, complimenting you before asking for a favor.

You deserve to be around people who respect you, not people who pressure, manipulate, or gaslight you. The more you trust yourself and your instincts, the easier it will be to stand up for what's right for you.

Being Social Is a Skill

Building strong social skills is about learning how to connect, communicate, and stand up for yourself. Whether you're setting boundaries, handling conflict, or just trying to read the room, these skills will help you in friendships, school, and even future jobs.

Not every interaction will go smoothly. Some might be downright embarrassing and awkward. The important thing is to **keep learning, keep growing, and remember that your voice and feelings matter**. Social skills take practice, but with time, they'll help you build relationships that are real, respectful, and good for you.

5

DIGITAL LIFE

Did you know that 96% of American teens say they use the Internet every day (Atske, 2024)?

The internet is a huge part of everyday life, even if you don't use it directly. It opens up a world of opportunities and experiences. But it also comes with **challenges**, like **staying safe** online, **avoiding comparison** traps, and making sure **screens don't take over your life**.

In this chapter, we'll talk about how to use technology in a way that works *for* you, not *against* you. That means setting healthy screen habits, understanding how influencers make money, spotting fake news, and knowing what happens to the things you post online.

P.S. If you don't have a phone or regular internet access, that's okay. This chapter will help prep you for the day you do.

Online Safety

You probably think of using the internet as scrolling through social media, watching YouTube, or gaming online. But the truth is, you probably use the internet in more ways than you realize. It's convenient and fun, which makes it easy to forget about the risks of using the internet.

PROTECTING YOUR PERSONAL DATA

Your full name, birthday, home address, and passwords are valuable. In the wrong hands, this information could put your accounts at risk of being hacked, or you could be tricked into giving someone money.

So, how do you keep data safe?

Use Strong Passwords

Your passwords should be **long and include numbers, letters, and symbols**. Don't use your name, birthday, or even a pet's name — this information is easy for people to find. Your password should be really hard to guess.

For example, *123456*, *password*, or *chocolate* are easy to guess, and hackers try these kinds of simple passwords first. On the other hand, *Giraffe$B3nch!92* uses a mix of uppercase and lowercase letters, numbers, and symbols, making it much harder to crack.

Never use the same password for different accounts or apps.

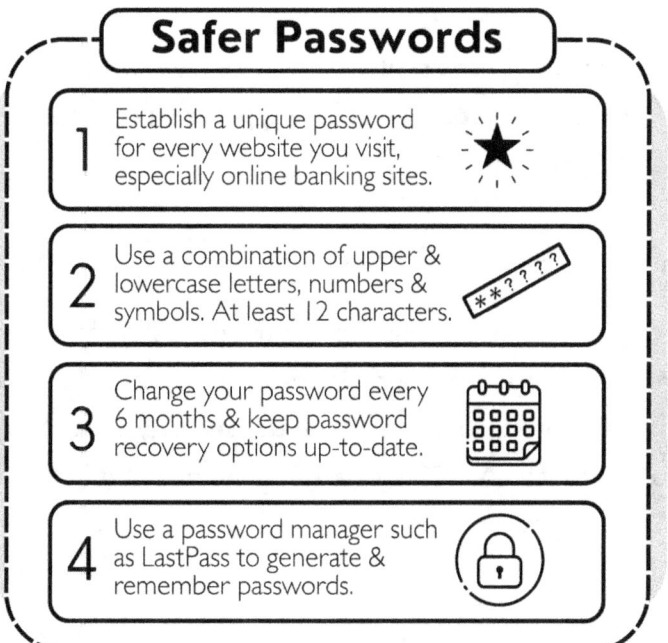

Use a passphrase instead of a single word. Something like PurpleTaco$Dance2024!. It's easier to remember than a meaningless string of characters, but it' still very strong.

Enable Two-Factor Authentication

Two-factor authentication (2FA) gives your accounts an extra layer of protection. Instead of just using a password to access an account, you need to complete a second step to prove it's really you. That step could be:

- **A one-time code** sent to your phone or email.
- A code from an **authenticator app** (like Google Authenticator).
- **A fingerprint** or **face scan.**

Check Your Privacy Settings

Many social media accounts have a public setting by default. That means anyone can see your pictures, videos, and information. You can make your accounts private in the security settings. A private account is much less likely to attract the attention of people who might want to do you harm.

PHISHING

Phishing is when scammers try to trick you into giving them personal information like passwords or credit card details by pretending to be someone trustworthy.

Common signs that you are being targeted include:

- **"Urgent" messages** or emails that try to get you to act quickly. They might say something like, "Your account has a problem! Click this link to fix it," or "You've won a prize! Click the link to claim it now."
- Messages with **links that look weird**, have spelling errors, or don't match the official website.
- Messages that have **spelling mistakes or bad grammar**.
- **Requests for personal details** like passwords or payment details over email or text.

The internet is an amazing tool, but it's also a place where you need to stay aware. When in doubt, **pause and think before you click** — a little caution now can save you a lot of trouble later!

Social Media

The legal age for using TikTok, Snapchat, Instagram, and Facebook is 13. But did you know that several countries, including Australia, are passing laws to introduce stricter social media controls for teens?

Social media has pros and cons. You can stay connected with friends or people you find interesting, express yourself, and learn new things. But you might also experience toxic interactions, get caught up in comparing yourself with others, or get drawn in by misinformation. Social media can also take up a lot of time and distract you from doing the things that really matter.

Think of social media as a theme park. It's full of rides, people, and loud voices. It can be fun and thrilling, but if you're not careful, you might get lost, overwhelmed, or find yourself on a scary ride. Just like in a theme park, it's important to **set limits**, **choose where you go** wisely, and **take breaks**. You should also understand that not everyone online is who they say they are, so be cautious when chatting with strangers or accepting requests from people you don't know.

How Influencers Make Money

Influencers have the power to affect the opinions, behaviors, or decisions of others, usually through social media. They share content, like pictures, videos, and posts, that often highlight a certain product or lifestyle "hack." You might follow an influencer because you like their style, advice, or personality.

Influencers don't just post for fun. They can have a huge impact on trends, and many **brands pay influencers to promote their products or services** to their followers. Sponsorship and paid content both involve brands paying influencers or creators, but they work slightly differently.

Sponsorship

This is when a brand teams up with an influencer to **promote their product or service**, but the influencer doesn't necessarily have to make the content themselves. The brand might give them the product and tell them how to show it off. For example, a clothing brand might sponsor a YouTuber to wear their clothes in a video or post a picture of them on Instagram. The influencer gets paid to promote the brand, but they might have to follow some guidelines on how they feature the product.

Paid Content

The influencer is paid to **create specific content**, like a review, tutorial, or shout-out, around a product or service. They usually have more freedom in how they present the content, but the key is they're still getting paid to talk about the brand. They might create something unique, but it's still all about promoting that product or service.

Affiliate Links

Influencers can also get a special link or discount code for brands or specific products. When you click on the link and buy a product, the influencer gets a percentage of the sale. There's nothing wrong with affiliate links, but **an influencer might push a product to make money** — even if it's not a good product or one they believe in.

Posts or videos that are **paid promotions** should use the **hashtag #ad** or clearly say that they are sponsored. If they don't, they're breaking the law.

Online Media

Online media includes websites, social media, blogs, podcasts, videos, news outlets, memes, and viral challenges. Pretty much anything you come across when you're browsing online counts as online media. It's constantly changing and evolving, and knowing **where your information comes from and how to spot credible sources is crucial**.

Biased or Fake News

Fake news is information that is **false or misleading**. It is often created to make people believe something that isn't true. It can spread quickly on social media or websites, especially if it's sensational or shocking.

Here's an example:

A headline might say, "*Scientists prove that eating pizza every day makes you smarter!*" Sounds great right?! But if there are no credible sources or scientific studies cited in the article to support the headline, the claim isn't backed by facts.

Not all misleading news is fake news. Some sources tell stories in a way that pushes certain opinions instead of just giving the facts. This is **biased news**. It might **leave out important information**, **twist the truth**, or use emotional language to try to get you to agree with a specific side.

Here's an example:

There are two articles about a new video game. One article is written by a gaming website that has a partnership with the game company, and it says, "***This game is a masterpiece and the best release of the year!***" The writer only talks about how awesome the graphics and gameplay are but doesn't mention any glitches or issues with the game.

On the other hand, a different article from an independent gaming site says, "*While the graphics are impressive,* ***the game has a lot of bugs*** *and doesn't live up to the hype.*"

You must get information from different sources, especially when the story is controversial. That way, you can compare how different sources talk about the same story.

SPOTTING MANIPULATION

Most internet content is designed to **grab your attention**, influence your opinions, or get you to buy things you often don't need. Sometimes, it's obvious, like an advert for a new video game. But other times, it's more subtle.

For example, imagine someone online posts a video raving about their **amazing new phone**. They don't **tell you to buy it**, but they make it seem like having this phone is the key to being **popular and cool**.

This is **subtle manipulation** because it's not a direct sales pitch. The video doesn't say, **"Buy this phone,"** but it **plants the idea** that if you don't have it, you're **missing out** or won't fit in. The influencer is using **peer pressure** without saying it outright, making you feel like this product is something you **"need"** — even though you probably don't.

Then, there are clickbait headlines.

"You Won't Believe What Happens Next — This Teen's Life Changed Forever After This One Decision!"

This headline is meant to **grab attention and make you curious**, but it doesn't really tell you what the story is about. It's designed to make you want to **click on it** to find the surprise, even though the content might not be as shocking or life-changing as it sounds. If a headline sounds **too good to be true** or exaggeratedly exciting, **it's probably clickbait.**

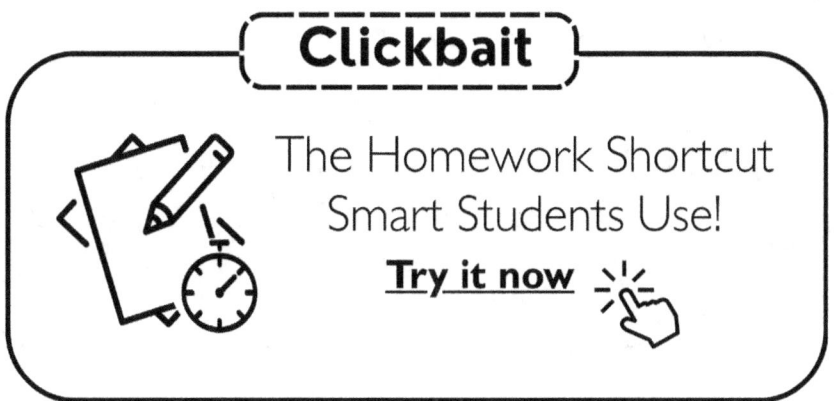

Your Digital Footprint

Everything you like, comment on, or post stays online long after you've moved on. A record of your online activity is **almost impossible to erase**. Even if you delete a post, there is a chance someone already took a screenshot or saved it.

Your digital footprint includes:

- **Social media** posts.
- **Comments** and messages.
- **Search history**.
- **Online accounts**.

Your digital footprint might not seem like a big deal now, but it could become one later in life. Schools, employers, and even sports recruiters check social media and online activity. Something that might seem funny or harmless to post now could be cringe-worthy or even damaging in a few years.

If you wouldn't be happy putting your name and face on a billboard with something you post online, don't post it.

Digital Kindness

The internet gives you access to the whole world, which is a crazy thought, right? But that much access and power comes with a lot of responsibility. Just like in the offline world, the way you treat people online matters.

Online interactions can uplift someone or tear them down. Whenever you interact online, you have the chance to be thoughtful, respectful, and understanding.

THINK BEFORE YOU TYPE

It's easy to fire off a comment or text behind a screen. But **words have power**.

Before you type, ask yourself:

- **Is this true?**
- **Is this necessary?**
- **Is this kind?**

If you wouldn't say something to someone's face, don't say it online. Remember, **a real person is on the other side of the screen** with feelings, thoughts, and opinions of their own.

Don't:

- ☒ **Make mean or sarcastic replies** to bullies. This can make the conflict worse.
- ☒ **Publicly call someone out**. Rather, message them privately if they have made a mistake.
- ☒ **Troll someone's account**. Being a troll means you post mean, annoying, or controversial comments online just to upset people or start arguments.

Artificial Intelligence

Artificial intelligence (AI) is everywhere. There are voice assistants like Siri and Alexa and chatbots like ChatGPT. Then there are the more subtle ways AI can show up in your life like Netflix or Spotify suggesting what to watch or listen to next. **AI is changing the way we search, create, and communicate**.

But what is AI, really?

AI is a technology that lets computers and machines do things that only humans were able to do in the past, like **understanding speech**, **recognizing patterns**, and **complex reasoning**. It uses huge amounts of data — pretty much everything that's online — to learn how to **solve problems**, make decisions, and even come up with ideas. You can use AI to generate images, answer questions, edit videos, and lots more.

Using AI

AI can be an amazing tool. But like all technology, you need to use it responsibly.

You can use AI to help you brainstorm or outline essays, but copying answers directly is not okay. AI can help you, but it can also make things too easy. Don't fall into the trap of **not thinking for yourself**.

AI can "hallucinate," which means it **makes things up** when it doesn't have the answer to a question. AI also learns from information that might be outdated, biased, or incorrect. You should always fact-check AI content.

AI is already making a big impact on the world around you, even if you don't always notice it. As the AI industry grows, it will play an even bigger role in shaping how we work, learn, and enjoy our free time.

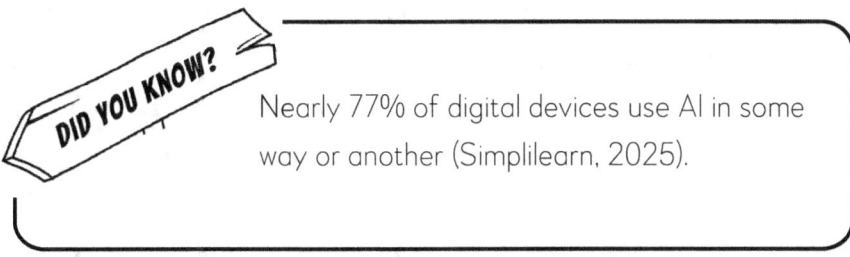

DID YOU KNOW? Nearly 77% of digital devices use AI in some way or another (Simplilearn, 2025).

Healthy Screen Habits

Phones, laptops, tablets, TVs, smartwatches, car screens, game consoles, billboards, and smart home screens are just some of the screens you might see every day. Screens have become a normal part of our lives, but using them too much can leave you exhausted, overwhelmed, and distracted. Here are some ways you can **practice healthy screen habits**.

Set Limits

It can be hard to say no to screen time sometimes. You can **set a timer** to allow yourself a certain amount of time to use screens. A screen time tracking app can tell you how much time you spend on your device. If you need extra help putting the screens away, some apps have a feature that lets you set a limit before locking the app.

Phones can keep you awake, so why not **set a bedtime for your phone outside your bedroom**? Some people think the blue light from devices can throw off your body clock, making it hard to fall asleep. Others think that it's the information on the phone that keeps you awake. Whichever it is, try to **stay off screens 30–60 minutes before bed** so your body can slip into sleep mode.

For even better sleep, **keep your phone out of your bedroom**.

> **Stop and Notice:** How many screens do you interact with in one day? You might be surprised (or shocked) at how many times screens appear in your day.

Don't Doomscroll

Doomscrolling is when you keep scrolling through negative news or videos, even though it makes you feel bad. The problem with doomscrolling is the more you do it, the more negativity you see, the worse you feel, and the more you doomscroll. It's a **vicious cycle**.

Social media uses algorithms that sort through tons of content and choose what it thinks you'll like most. It does this by looking at:

- What you like, comment on, share, or watch all the way through.
- Posts from friends or accounts you interact with often.
- Trends and popular content that people are engaging with.

Their goal is to keep you scrolling, trapping you in a "bubble" of similar content. Think about this when you're interacting with social media content — what do you want more of in your feed? What would you like to see less of?

If you start noticing content that makes you **uncomfortable**, most platforms allow you to **delete your history and reset the algorithm** to refresh what appears in your feed.

Use Screen Time Wisely

It's almost impossible to avoid screens, but if you have healthy screen habits, you won't need to. **Instead of doomscrolling or comparing yourself to someone else's highlight reel, why not learn something new?**

There are loads of resources online that can help you **learn a new skill** or explore your interests, or better still step away from the screen and head to the library to read a book!

When you interact with positive content, you can curate what you see online and create a more positive space that inspires you.

You'll enjoy your online time more when you have control over it.

Taking Control of Your Digital World

The digital world is important, and how you use it matters. You have the power to **make smart choices, protect your privacy, and use technology in a way that benefits you instead of controlling you**. Social media, AI, and online trends will keep evolving, but one thing stays the same: you're in charge of your digital life. Set boundaries, think before you click, and use the internet to grow, not just scroll.

BIG-PICTURE THINKING

Life is busy and it's easy to get caught up in everyday stuff like homework, friend drama, and weekend plans. But have you ever stopped to zoom out and think about what your life might look like in a few years?

What kind of person do you want to be?
What excites you?
What's worth your time and energy?

Big-picture thinking helps you **see the "why" behind your actions**. It helps you make choices that matter rather than reacting to whatever's in front of you. Zooming out helps you understand that success isn't just about grades and that the future isn't as scary as it might seem.

You should **live in the moment** and **soak up all the experiences** that come with being a teenager. But that doesn't mean you can't carve out space to consider the type of life you want to lead and the person you want to be.

Why School Isn't Everything

School probably feels like a **big deal** because it takes up so much of your time. You're told to **study hard, get good grades, aim for college, and follow your dreams** — and honestly? That's great advice.

Finishing school and working hard for **the best grades you can get** is often the **first step toward success**. It doesn't guarantee you'll be rich, but **dropping out can make life much harder**.

People who don't finish school are more likely to struggle with finding stable jobs, earning enough money, and having the freedom to choose what they want to do. **Education matters**, and school can be a great place to learn, grow, and have experiences that set you up for later success. Even if your dream job doesn't require a diploma, **having a solid foundation will give you more options**. That's what real success is about.

That said, **school isn't the only path to success**. Just ask Jimmy Donaldson aka. Mr. Beast, who dropped out of college after two weeks and now has a billion-dollar empire that he started with a YouTube channel. But here's the thing — he spent years studying YouTube, algorithms, and content creation before that happened. **He took growing his business as seriously as he would have taken studying** something he was really passionate about.

Grades Only Go So Far

Grades measure how well you do in school, but **they don't define how smart, creative, or capable you are**. Some of the most successful people in the world struggled in school. There are plenty of examples of artists, musicians, athletes, entrepreneurs, and tech gurus who found success outside of traditional education. Steve Jobs and Mark Zuckerberg dropped out of college, while Taylor Swift didn't attend at all.

Success Doesn't Look the Same for Everyone

Some people thrive in a classroom while others learn best by doing. Maybe they like working with people or building things. These kinds of skills matter just as much as acing a test.

School helps you gain knowledge and gives you opportunities like playing sports or interacting with different people. But you don't have to fit into the "perfect student" mold to be successful.

Setting Goals That Matter

Goals are not just things you complete to check off a list. They let you turn something that excites you into something real.

Here's an example:

If you are passionate about the environment, you might start by reducing waste and recycling at home. A bigger goal could be organizing a cleanup or educating others. These **small steps are building skills** that could eventually lead to a job, maybe in environmental research or creating eco-friendly products.

The best goals are the ones that **get you excited** rather than the ones other people set for you.

But how do you know what goals to set?

Notice the things that light you up. Do you love writing stories or coding? Or maybe you design clothes or volunteer at the local animal shelter. Your passions form the foundation for goals that mean something to you.

SMART Goals

The SMART goals framework makes setting goals easy because it gives you simple steps to follow.

SMART goals are: **S**pecific, **M**easurable, **A**chievable, **R**elevant, **T**imebound

Here's an example:
Original goal: I want to get better at art.

Now, let's make it SMART.

- **Specific:** Instead of just saying you want to get better at art, be more specific by **focusing on one element** like drawing more realistic portraits.

- **Measurable:** You can **track your progress** by drawing one new portrait each week and noticing how your skills improve.
- **Achievable:** Do you have the basic art **skills** needed for drawing portraits? Is sketching faces something you can get better at with practice? If so, this is an achievable goal. If not, maybe you need to break the goal down and tackle it in parts.
- **Relevant:** Why is this goal **important to you**? Maybe you have an art project at school or you want to give your mom a portrait for her birthday.
- **Timebound:** The goal needs a **deadline** so you have something to work towards and keep you motivated.

So, the SMART version of this goal might be: I will **improve** my **portraiture before my mom's birthday** by drawing **one portrait a week**, and give my best portrait to her as a gift.

Breaking Down Goals

Goals, especially big ones, can feel overwhelming. The SMART goals framework is a great first step. But how could we make the goal feel easier to achieve? One way is to **break big goals down into several smaller ones**.

So, if the goal is to get better at drawing faces, you might break that down into smaller steps to make it happen:

1. Gather supplies like pencils and a sketchpad.

2. Choose a reference photo.
3. Practice sketching basic shapes, like eyes, ears, or nostrils.
4. Practice getting the proportions right.
5. Add shading and depth.

Breaking goals into smaller steps can help you take **consistent steps** toward reaching them.

Values and Ethics

Values act like an internal compass that guides your actions. They help you make decisions based on what's important to you and the kind of person you want to be. Values can vary quite a lot between different people, and we develop them over time through thinking carefully about our priorities.

For example, when you choose to spend your spare time playing sports or shopping, you're showing which activity is more important to you — which you **value** more. Values can also be passed on **through families** or other groups. It's important to think critically about what values you have, where they came from, and whether they still reflect who you are.

Ethics are another type of "guidance system," which helps you tell right from wrong. They're usually set by the society you live in and most of the time they don't vary much between individual people. **Your ethics are what help you to do the morally right thing**, even when no one is looking. For example, if you found a wallet on the floor full of cash, what would you do? No one would know if you took the money. Would you keep it or hand it in? Why?

Your values and ethics aren't just about big choices — it's the **small decisions** you make **every day** that determine the kind of person you are. Sometimes, making the right decision isn't simple. There are times when doing the right thing is complicated and inconvenient. Occasionally, it might be hard to see what the right thing to do even is. But if you know the kind of person you want to be, making the right choice is easier.

Here are some common ethical dilemmas that you might face.

CHEATING

Have you ever forgotten your homework and thought about copying from your friend? Or maybe you were unprepared for a test and tried to look over at your neighbor's paper. You know that **cheating is wrong**, but the temptation to do it can be strong. **Cheating is a pointless shortcut** that has serious consequences — **you don't**

learn anything, your self-respect will take a hit, and you risk losing other people's trust and respect too.

Lying

Lying might seem like the easy way out when you want to avoid conflict or getting into trouble. **Lies often start small** — ever said you've finished your homework when you haven't? But they have a way of spiraling. **One small lie often leads to more and more lies.** Soon, you've broken the trust of the people around you and lost plenty of self-respect too. Honesty can be uncomfortable or embarrassing, but it builds character and stronger relationships.

Snitching vs. Speaking Up

The line between speaking up for what's right and "telling" can feel blurry. You might not want to be seen as the tattle-tale, but sometimes, you know that what is happening is wrong. **If someone is in danger** or could be seriously hurt (emotionally or physically), **speaking up is the right thing to do.** But think hard before telling on someone for something unimportant, just because you want to get them in trouble. Your values will help you decide what the right thing to do is.

Peer Pressure

People might try to pressure you into doing something risky like drinking, vaping, shoplifting, or sneaking out of the house at night. You might be tempted, even if you know it's wrong. But making choices based on pleasing other people rather than your values often leads to regret. No one can make you do anything — **you have the power to choose your actions**. Always follow your values and do what *you* think is right.

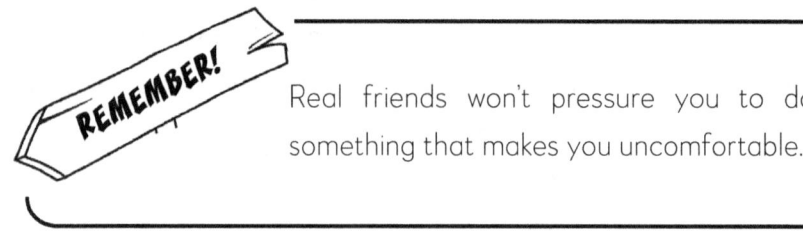

REMEMBER! Real friends won't pressure you to do something that makes you uncomfortable.

Covering for a Friend

Has a friend ever asked you to cover for them so they didn't get into trouble? It's a difficult situation because you want to be a loyal friend and protect them. However, **lying for them can hurt you**. Remember how one lie usually leads to another and eats away at your self-respect? That's no good for anyone. Supporting your friends shouldn't mean getting wrapped up in their bad decisions.

GOSSIPING

Sharing a piece of juicy gossip with a friend can be fun, right? But have you ever considered the damage spreading rumors can do? **Gossip can hurt friendships and reputations.** Sharing something you heard might make you feel popular and powerful in the moment, but that brief feeling is at someone else's expense. Would you want people sharing details about you behind your back?

> **Values: Questions to Ask Yourself:**
> *Would I feel fine if everyone knew I did this?*
> *Will I be proud of this choice later?*
> *How would I feel if someone did this to me?*

Understanding Citizenship

What country are you a citizen of? What does that mean to you? Did you know that citizenship is more than just living in a country? There are a few things that come as part of the deal. Being a citizen means:

- **Being** part of the community.
- **Understanding** how your choices, actions, and voice matter.
- **Using** your voice and power responsibly.

You might not be old enough to vote yet, but this is the perfect time to learn what it means to be a citizen and how society works.

WHAT IS CITIZENSHIP?

A citizen is a member of a country who has certain rights and responsibilities. You can be born a citizen, or gain citizenship by moving to a country and meeting certain requirements. Although citizenship explains someone's legal status in a country, it's also about **how they participate in the community**, use their voice, and **treat others**.

VOTING

Voting is one of the biggest ways people shape their country. It isn't just a right — **it's a responsibility**. The legal voting age in most countries is 18.

The people who get elected make decisions about things like education, the environment, jobs, and even the internet — **things that shape the world you're growing up in**. Laws about school funding, climate policies, or the minimum wage for your first job are all decided by people who were voted into office.

Even though you can't vote yet, the adults around you are choosing leaders who will shape the world you'll live in when you're old enough to work, drive, and go to college.

Policies made today could impact:

- **Your education** (school funding, class sizes, what's taught in history, science, and other subjects).
- **Your future job opportunities** (minimum wage, internships, career programs).
- **Your freedoms** (laws about social media, personal rights, or safety rules).

Getting Involved

You don't have to wait for 18 to **get involved in the world around you**. There are plenty of ways to get a head start!

Pay Attention to Current Events

Even if politics seems boring, **find a topic that matters to you** (like climate change or mental health resources for teens) and follow how leaders are handling it.

Think Critically About News and Social Media

Politicians, the media, and influencers push a lot of information — some of it true, some of it misleading, some of it false. Practicing fact-checking now will **help you make informed choices later**.

Talk to Adults Who Vote

Ask your parents, teachers, or other adults why they vote and **what issues matter to them**. Hearing different perspectives helps you think about what's important to you and build your value system.

Understanding Laws

Laws help keep people safe and **create a society that is orderly and just**. Right now, the law might feel like something that just happens to you, but soon enough, you'll be able to vote and advocate for causes that mean something to you.

Even though you're not writing laws or voting on them yet, they still impact you.

- Laws decide how schools handle things like bullying, dress codes, and your right to a safe learning environment.
- There are laws about data privacy, cyberbullying, and what companies can do with your personal information.
- Laws protect things like free speech, but they also set limits. For example, hate speech or discrimination isn't protected.

Ask questions! If something seems unfair, dig deeper. Why does a rule exist? Who benefits from it? Who decides if it stays or changes? Critical thinking is key to understanding the bigger picture.

Responsibilities of a Good Citizen

Being a good citizen is **more than just following the rules**. As a citizen, you have certain responsibilities that help shape the world around you. Your values and those of the communities you belong to will have an impact on your responsibilities, but here are a few that apply to all of us:

- **Respect others**, even if you don't agree with their opinions or choices.
- **Stay informed** so you understand different perspectives and issues around you.
- **Get involved** by volunteering and supporting causes you believe in.
- **Take responsibility** for your actions, be honest, and stand up for what's right.
- **Be a smart shopper** by supporting brands that care about the planet and their employees.
- **Hold leaders accountable** by asking questions and writing letters to your representatives.

Privilege

Life isn't a level playing field. Some people start out with more advantages (like money, education, connections, and access to opportunities) than others. Privilege means having certain benefits that not everyone gets, even if you didn't ask for them.

Privilege isn't something to feel guilty about, but it is something to **recognize and use wisely**. Some people think that having privilege means your life is easy. This isn't always true. However, privilege does mean that certain challenges might not affect you as much as others.

For example:
- You might not have to think about having a **safe home** or **enough food**.
- Maybe **you can go to school** without worrying about working to support your family or care for a sick relative.
- You might not have to consider whether a place is **accessible** for you.

It's important to be aware that others may face struggles you don't have and use that awareness to be **kinder**, more **responsible**, and more **understanding**.

Privilege and Responsibility

When you have privilege, you should use what you have to help, not harm:

- **Speak up** when you see injustice or unfairness.
- **Learn about different perspectives** and listen to others' experiences.

- **Use your resources** to help when you can.
- **Be aware of how your choices impact other people** and the environment.

Think of privilege as having a flashlight in a dark room full of people who are all trying to find the door. You can ignore the people struggling in the shadows and quickly make your way to the door alone, or you can **use your advantage to help light the way for others**.

Independence vs. Rules

You might feel some pushing and pulling as you get older and start to question the rules around you. You may start wanting and needing more freedom, but you'll still have to follow certain rules — it can be frustrating. It could feel like you're ready to make your choices, but the adults in your life keep stepping in.

But independence doesn't mean breaking the rules and getting to do what you want when you want. It's about **learning to handle responsibility** so you can eventually set your own rules.

Why Do Rules Exist?

Rules **keep you safe and help you develop good habits**. They can be frustrating but try to look at them through a bigger lens and understand how they can **help you grow** into the kind of person you want to be. For example:

- **Curfews** exist to make sure you're **home safe** and getting enough sleep. They can help you make good choices when you're older and stay in control of your own schedule.
- **Rules at school** help create a space where **people can learn** without distractions.
- Doing **household chores** can **teach you to be responsible** and help you develop important skills you'll need when you leave home.

Earning Independence

Independence isn't about doing what you want. It's about proving that you can **handle the responsibility** that comes with more freedom. Instead of fighting against the rules, why not **think about how you can show that you're ready for more freedom**?

Show You Can Be Trusted

Follow the rules without complaining. When you consistently stick with the boundaries you're given, you show that you can be trusted.

Take the Initiative

Do your homework without being asked, help out at home, and plan your schedule responsibly. **Show that you can handle more freedom** and still do the important things you need to.

Be Ready to Compromise

If changing the rules isn't an option, see if there is some middle ground. For example, if you want a 10 pm curfew and your parents say no, you could ask to stay out until 9:30 pm if you agree to check in at 8:30 pm and again at 9 pm.

Communicate

Rules might not always seem fair. Rather than arguing though, try **talking respectfully** about it.

- **Ask for the reason** behind the rule. It might make more sense when you understand the other person's perspective.
- Give examples of how you've been responsible and why you think the rule should change.
- **Ask for a trial run** by introducing a new (adjusted) rule to prove you can handle the responsibility.

Independence is about making smart decisions when no one is telling you what to do. It's something you need to earn, proving that you are ready for more freedom.

Seeing the Bigger Picture

Big-picture thinking isn't about having all the answers right now. It's about understanding that **life is bigger than today's challenges.** Your grades, friendships, and daily choices all matter, but they're pieces of a much larger puzzle.

The world is full of possibilities, and your choices now will help you build a future that reflects your passions, values, and dreams. Use what you know to **keep learning, keep growing, and keep making a positive impact on the world** around you.

CONCLUSION

So, have you thought much about your future? Or does it still feel like something **far off in the distance?**

The future is full of **unknowable mysteries, waiting to unfold** one day. But much of what **your future** will look like **is down to the choices you're making now,** and those you'll make in the next few years.

In this book, you've explored everything from handling emotions and conflict to managing money, setting goals, and thinking about the future. You've learned how to set boundaries, spot manipulation, navigate the digital world, and develop real-world skills that will help you in life. But no book can cover everything, and **life will always throw new challenges** your way. **Don't worry — you've got this!**

Growing up isn't about having all the answers (what fun would life be if you did?) The whole point of growing up is trying new things, learning new skills, and figuring out who you are and what you like along the way. One of the biggest lessons you can take with you is that **you have control over the kind of person you become**. Every choice you make, the habits you build, and the challenges you face help shape your future. **Mistakes will happen**. Bad days will come. But **how you respond to those moments makes all the difference**.

Remember, **success isn't just about getting good grades or making money**. It's about building a life that feels meaningful to you. So, **be kind, stay curious, surround yourself with good people, and never stop learning**.

APPENDIX

1. Achievement, J., USA. (2023, August 10). *New research shows the majority of teens feel unprepared to finance their futures.* Junior Achievement USA. https://jausa.ja.org/news/press-releases/new-research-shows-the-majority-of-teens-feel-unprepared-to-finance-their-futures

2. Atske, S. (2024, December 11). Teens and Internet, Device Access Fact sheet. *Pew Research Center.* https://www.pewresearch.org/internet/fact-sheet/teens-and-internet-device-access-fact-sheet/

3. Lau, J. (2020, September 11). Google Maps 101: How AI helps predict traffic and determine routes. *Google.* https://blog.google/products/maps/google-maps-101-how-ai-helps-predict-traffic-and-determine-routes/

4. Quizlet. (2024, March 27). Quizlet Survey Reveals Students Crave Life Skills Education. *PR Newswire.* https://www.prnewswire.com/news-releases/quizlet-survey-reveals-students-crave-life-skills-education-302100754.html

5. Simplilearn. (2025, February 12). *Top artificial intelligence stats you should know about in 2025.* Simplilearn.com. https://www.simplilearn.com/artificial-intelligence-stats-article

6. Van Edwards, V. (2025, January 26). *The Definitive Guide to Reading Microexpressions (Facial Expressions).* Science of People. https://www.scienceofpeople.com/microexpressions/

THANKS
FOR READING MY
BOOK!

I truly hope you enjoyed the book and that the content is valuable now and in the future.

I would be grateful if you could leave an honest review or a star rating on Amazon.
(A star rating is just a couple of clicks away.)

By leaving a review, you'll help other parents discover this valuable resource for their children. Thank you!

To leave a review & help spread the word

SCAN HERE

www.ingramcontent.com/pod-product-compliance
Lightning Source LLC
Chambersburg PA
CBHW071207070526
44584CB00019B/2946